THE BIRTH OF
BLACK AMERICA

PRINCE HENRY
OF
PORTUGALL

HONI SOIT QVI MAL Y PENSE

CEUTA

THE BIRTH OF BLACK AMERICA

THE AGE OF DISCOVERY AND THE SLAVE TRADE

Andrew K. Frank

CHELSEA HOUSE PUBLISHERS
New York   Philadelphia

FRONTISPIECE Prince Henry the Navigator stands boldly before the town of Ceuta in North Africa. According to one chronicler, at Henry's birth the stars foretold that he would "engage in great and noble conquests, and . . . attempt the discovery of things which were hidden from other men."

ON THE COVER Captured West Africans battle for their freedom aboard the slaver *Amistad* in 1839. At least 50 such mutinies took place during the years of the slave trade.

Chelsea House Publishers
Editorial Director   Richard Rennert
Executive Managing Editor   Karyn Gullen Browne
Copy Chief   Robin James
Picture Editor   Adrian G. Allen
Creative Director   Robert Mitchell
Art Director   Joan Ferrigno
Production Manager   Sallye Scott

Milestones in Black American History
Senior Editor   Marian W. Taylor
Series Originator and Adviser   Benjamin I. Cohen
Series Consultants   Clayborne Carson, Darlene Clark Hine

Staff for THE BIRTH OF BLACK AMERICA
Associate Editor   Mary B. Sisson
Assistant Editor   Annie McDonnell
Senior Designer   Cambraia Magalhães
Picture Researcher   Toby Greenberg

First Printing

1 3 5 7 9 8 6 4 2

Library of Congress Cataloging-in-Publication Data

Frank, Andrew.
    The birth of black America: the Age of Discovery and the slave trade/Andrew Frank.
      p. cm.—(Milestones in Black American history)
    Includes bibliographical references (p.) and index.
    Summary: A history of early exploration in the Americas and Africa and an examination of the slave trade that followed.
    ISBN 0-7910-2257-9
    ISBN 0-7910-2683-3 (pbk.)
1. Slave trade—History—Juvenile literature. 2. Slave trade—Africa—History—Juvenile literature. 3. America—Discovery and exploration—Juvenile literature. 4. Conquerors—America—History—Juvenile literature. 5. Conquerors—Africa—History—Juvenile literature. [1. Slave trade—History. 2. America—Discovery and exploration. 3. Explorers.] I. Title. II. Series.
HT975.F73 1996   95-310038
352'.44—dc20   CIP
                                                                          AC

CONTENTS

MILESTONES IN BLACK AMERICAN HISTORY

INTRODUCTION

In the 15th century, Renaissance Europe began to revitalize its culture and shed the superstitions of the Middle Ages. At the same time, Africa and Asia's ancient civilizations continued to flourish. Europeans glimpsed the splendor of these distant societies through the exotic spices, jewels, and precious metals offered by North African and Arab traders. Eager to expand their role in this profitable trade, far-sighted leaders—among them the Portuguese prince known as Henry the Navigator—launched a series of seagoing explorations, thereby inaugurating the Age of Discovery.

One of these expeditions sparked the birth of African American history, a saga of courage and cruelty, of horror and glory, of bitter defeat and blood-pounding excitement and triumph. The story starts more than 550 years ago, when a Portuguese sailing vessel returned to port with an extraordinary cargo: 12 African captives, who were sold at a Portuguese market. Africans had been enslaving each other for centuries, but their form of bondage was vastly different from that developed by the Europeans. After faithfully serving their African masters, slaves were often allowed to own land, marry, and raise free children. But under European domination, the slave trade developed into a far more inhumane and cruel institution, one in which masters treated their people as property, not as fellow human beings.

The European slave trade remained limited in scale until explorer Christopher Columbus sailed west from Spain and landed in the Americas. Soon realizing that exploiting the New World's riches would require intensive labor, European settlers tried to recruit Native American workers, but with little success. The settlers then began to import laborers kidnapped from Africa, justifying their actions by citing religion: "heathen" Africans would be converted to Christianity for their own good. Slavery's true motivation, however, was economic: the practice made white traders and plantation owners wealthy, and it gave black slave merchants European weapons and enhanced power.

In the 1600s, more European nations seized colonies in the New World and entered the booming slave trade. The first Africans arrived in the American colonies in 1619—a year before the Pilgrims landed at Plymouth—and legions more followed. As slavery became an integral part of the colonies' economic success, its practitioners entrenched it with the myth of white superiority and with laws that discriminated against blacks.

Racism and greed spawned an institution of shocking cruelty. More than 10 million Africans were kidnapped and shipped to the New World, enduring inhumane conditions each step of the way. After trekking to Africa's west coast in shackles, captives faced the Middle Passage, a long voyage in overcrowded, filthy ships where disease and malnutrition killed up to a third of the passengers. Survivors, often deliberately separated from their families, were then sold on the auction block to masters who frequently inflicted brutal beatings and demanded backbreaking labor.

Despite harsh treatment, many captives displayed astonishing courage and resilience. Slaves organized more than 50 mutinies and countless smaller, unrecorded uprisings, and many escaped, establishing their own communities in the mountains. In 1791, rebellious slaves overthrew their masters and established the independent black nation of Haiti. Steadfast African American resistance, backed by the crusading whites who loathed the system, undermined the slave system and eventually led to the abolition of the slave trade; Great Britain outlawed it in 1807, the United States a year later. U.S. slavery finally ended altogether in 1865, following the Union victory in the Civil War.

The United States is still grappling with the consequences of this trade in human cargo, but early African Americans left a positive legacy for future generations to build on. Africans explored the New World alongside European trailblazers, and they provided the engine for the American colonies' economic growth. Overcoming enormous odds, Africans carved out a home in the New World, preserving elements of their language, religion, and traditions and immeasurably enriching American culture.

MILESTONES
1419–1865

1419   • Prince Henry the Navigator establishes an exploration center in Sagres, Portugal, to gather geographical and maritime information and to devise new navigational instruments and seagoing vessels. Over the next several years, Henry creates updated maps and oversees the development of the caravel, a small, fast cargo ship. In addition, the prince launches numerous expeditions to explore the western African coast and its offshore islands in search of a sea route around the bottom of Africa to the markets of the East.

1441   • One of Prince Henry's ships returns from Africa with 12 captives. The Africans are sold at Lagos, Portugal, for a tidy profit, sparking interest in a potential slave trade.

1444   • Henry dispatches an expedition to Africa's western coast specifically to bring back human cargo. Europeans gradually establish ties with African slave merchants, and the slave trade begins in earnest. A portion of the slaves work in Europe as domestic servants, farmers, and craftspeople, but most labor on colonial sugarcane plantations.

1487   • Portuguese explorer Bartolomeu Dias de Novais reaches the southern tip of Africa by sea.

1492   • Searching for a new route to India, Christopher Columbus sails west from Spain and lands in the Caribbean. He returns to Spain with a glowing report of the New World and its stunning wealth in gold and free Indian labor.

1499   • Vasco de Gama sails around the African continent to the Indian subcontinent and back again, opening trade between Portugal and Asia. British, Dutch, and French traders enter the African trade, initially focusing on precious metals and spices rather than slaves.

1515
- Father Bartolomé de Las Casas campaigns against the enslavement of Native Americans and suggests that Europeans or Africans provide labor in Spanish colonies.

1518
- The Spanish crown authorizes the first direct shipment of slaves from Africa to the Americas.

1526
- Mani-Congo Nzinga Mbemba, ruler of the Congo empire, attempts to end the slave trade but is stripped of power by his own nobles; the profits and the weapons gained from the slave trade motivate many Africans to cooperate with the European slavers.

1539
- Estevanico (or Estevanillo), a North African, leads the first Spanish expedition into the American Southwest and meets his death at the hands of hostile Native Americans. Many Africans play important roles in the Spanish exploration and conquest of the New World.

1572
- Diego, a runaway African slave, assists English seaman Francis Drake in raiding Spanish settlements and transport ships. Diego, who directs other free blacks in helping the English cause, also acts as Drake's valued personal assistant.

1595
- Spain begins granting the *asiento*, a permit for a foreign trader to ship a certain number of slaves to its colonies in Central and South America. As merchants from more European countries acquire the asiento, the slave trade becomes a booming industry.

1619
- A Dutch ship lands in Jamestown, Virginia, and sells 20 African captives, the first blacks in the North American colonies.

1645
- Massachusetts authorities arrest two slave merchants and return their captives to Africa because the traders had violated a law against kidnapping and selling men. The distinction between stealing men and trading slaves is extremely slight, though, and the law is not enforced again.

1648
- African slaves teach Virginia settlers how to convert marshland into profitable rice fields. The slaves' knowledge and labor provide the engine for economic development in the New World.

1664
- Maryland adopts the first antimiscegenation law, which bans interracial relationships. By the early 1700s, Virginia, Massachusetts, North Carolina, South Carolina, and Delaware have also imposed harsh punishments for intermarriage.

1667
- Virginia decrees that conversion to Christianity does not change a slave's status, and other colonies soon pass similar laws. Race, rather than religion, becomes the defining factor of who can be enslaved.

1676
- Virginian Nathaniel Bacon leads a group of poor, discontented whites in a revolt against the colonial governor. Fearing further such unrest, Virginia's government encourages the importation of African slaves instead of British indentured servants.

1706
- Bostonian Cotton Mather, an influential Protestant clergyman, writes *The Negro Christianized*, which provides religious justification for the enslavement of "heathen" Africans and Native Americans.

1736
- Suspecting a plot for revolt, white Antiguans torture slave leaders until they incriminate themselves and others; 88 blacks are executed during the crisis.

1776
- The American colonies sever ties with Great Britain. Thomas Jefferson attempts to include a condemnation of the British slave trade in the Declaration of Independence but southern delegates to the Continental Congress object.

1781
- Luke Collingwood, captain of the British slave ship *Zong*, chains together and throws overboard 133 sick slaves to collect insurance. Collingwood is never charged with a crime, but his action greatly increases antislavery sentiment in England.

1787
- Concerned Britons found the Society for Effecting the Abolition of the Slave Trade and raise public awareness of the trade's brutality.

1791
- Toussaint L'Ouverture leads a slave rebellion in the French colony Santo Domingo and spurs the creation of Haiti, the first independent black nation in the West.

1807
- England becomes the first nation to abolish the African slave trade. The United States joins the ban the following year, but pirates from England and other nations continue the trade for several more decades.

1820
- Under pressure from England, Spain agrees to abolish its slave trade.

1839
- Captured African Cinque leads a revolt aboard the slaver *Amistad*. After subduing the ship's crew, the Africans sail to New York, where they are captured and tried. Cleared and released, they return to Africa in 1841. Although more than 50 organized mutinies occur during the years of the slave trade, few succeed; hunger strikes and suicides are also common.

1840s
- The British navy attacks Brazilian slavers; resenting such interference, officials often aid illegal slave traders.

1865
- The Civil War ends, and the 13th Amendment outlaws slavery in the United States.

Oceanus
Austro
Soffala
Etiopia Australe
Fl. Galla
Ethyopia
Mare Indicum
Siroco
Etiopia Occidentale
Saba
Abassia
Adel
Ifat
Cetoschamar
Garamantia
Fundan
Sumatra
Mare Indicum
Cholecut
Mare Persicum
Malabar
Guzirat
Arabia Felice
Sinus Ethiopicus
Merot
Palude
Fl. Nilo
Nuba
Maoritania
Garamantia
Deserto
M. Atlante
Arabia
Thasi
Deserto
Persia
Susiana
Deserta Petrea
Deli
India Prima
Cremania
Lago
India Seconda
India Terza
Cina
Phison
Tebet
Persia
Babilonia
Caldea
Media
Asiria
Judea
Siria
Egypto
Libia
Cirenaica
Fessa
Marocho
Numidia
Atlanticus
Gaditaneum
Mare Mediteraneum
Damasco
Asia minor
Monte Thauro
Armenia
Balach
Chorasia
Spahan
Thauris
Soltania
Pontus Euxinus
Macedonia
Servia
Crovatia
Italia
Sardenia
Ispania
Gallia
Fl. Ren
Bolgaria
Alemagna
Danubio
Ungaria
Anglia
Scotia
Oceanus
Mare Breunto
M. Imaus
Zenguy
P. Sace
Tangui
Deserto
Serica
Lop
Balsh
Zagatai
Mar Chaspio
Chaspio
Tartaria
Fl. Tanai
Polana
Praga
Prusia
Chatajo
Zouza
Insical
Samargant
Orgaria
Sarey
P. Gothan
Otrar
Fl. Edil
Rossia Rossa
Lituana
Riga
Norvegia
Svetia
Rossia Negra
Rossia Biancha
Alana
Novograd
Rossia
Filandia
Islant
Chatajo
Xandu
Tangut
Sitbia
Mar Biancha
P. Destini
Dislana
P. Sibir
P. Nef
P. Balimata
P. Meschiera
Permia
Permia
P. Cestan
Septentrio
Tramontana
Sepolcro Uncam
M. Altai
Gambaleck
Templum Sepulture

1

DISCOVERY AND AFRICA

From the 15th to the 18th century, a time later known as the Age of Discovery, the people of Europe undertook a series of remarkable expeditions, exploring the world's seas and continents. Bold, intrepid, and eager for wealth, European adventurers set out in tiny ships across vast and dangerous seas in search of new lands and new people. What they discovered led to a bright prospect: expanding international markets and communications. It also led to a dark reality: a far-reaching trade network whose sole purpose was the purchase, transportation, and resale of captured Africans.

Some historians date the Age of Discovery from the 15th-century Portuguese incursions into Africa, but contact between Africa and Europe actually began far earlier. People have lived on the African continent for thousands of years; archaeological evidence indicates that the ancestors of the Europeans (and of all humans) originally came from Africa. Northern Africans and southern Europeans have traded, communi-

A mid-15th-century Portuguese map reflects the limits of European geographical knowledge at the dawn of the Age of Discovery. The map accurately depicts the area around the Mediterranean Sea, but Asia and Africa are more vague, and Australia and the Americas do not appear at all. (Unlike contemporary maps, this one is oriented so that the south is at the top of the page.)

cated, fought, and worked together for centuries. The African state of Egypt was an important province of both the Greek and Roman empires, and many of the classical Greek and Roman philosophers and scientists, men who deeply influenced European thought, were probably African, residents of the Egyptian city of Alexandria.

Indeed, the Age of Discovery was sparked by a conflict between neighboring Africans and Europeans. In the 8th century, the Iberian Peninsula in southwestern Europe was conquered by a group of Muslim North Africans known as the Moors. (Muslims are practitioners of the religion of Islam, which centers around the teachings of the prophet Mohammed.) During the 11th century, the Christian Iberians began the long, slow process of driving out their conquerors, eventually establishing two kingdoms: Portugal in the 12th century and Spain in the 15th century. Relations between the Moors and their former vassals were far from cordial, each side frequently attacking the other. The situation was worsened by the religious differences between the fiercely Christian Europeans and their equally single-minded Muslim African counterparts. Although the two cultures maintained trade links, the constant hostilities meant that very few Europeans actually ever visited Africa.

Although they stayed close to home, Europeans hungered for the products of the exotic lands they would never see. High on the list were such condiments as pepper, cinnamon, nutmeg, and cloves, which refused to grow in the temperate climate of Europe. Because the Europeans paid well for these

This engraving depicts the different types of sailing vessels used by 15th-century Portuguese mariners as they plied the seas. Despite such advanced sailing technology, long ocean journeys—especially expeditions to the uncharted shores of southern Africa—were fraught with danger.

delicacies, those who imported them could earn not only great wealth but great power.

For centuries, merchants from the Italian coastal cities of Genoa and Venice had been trading with the Arab market centers in Egypt and Syria, principally for spices that Arab traders had brought back from the East. Controlling a trade monopoly, the two port cities had flourished, a prosperity that rankled the rest of Europe's commercial world. Rather than trying to compete directly with the Genoans and Venetians, other southern Europeans began to consider a new trade route to the spice-laden East—a water path that would bypass Venice, Genoa, and the Arabs altogether. The search for a route to that wealth opened the Age of Discovery, an era that eventually witnessed the European colonization of North and South America, Africa, Asia, and Australia. From these distant points, spices, silks, jewels, ivory, gold, jade, and other exotic goods flowed into the European kingdoms, vastly increasing their power and prestige.

Sailing around Africa, however, presented enormous challenges. The most serious arose from the lack of information—and the mass of misinformation—about Africa itself. Because the waters surrounding the continent had never been charted, seamen had nothing to guide them but day-to-day observations and ancient legends. No European captain knew how far south the African continent extended, and none knew whether its inhabitants were friendly or hostile.

Fifteenth-century seamen were rich sources of the myths and horror stories that spring from fear of the unknown. In Africa, they said, dragons and monsters abounded; raging fires covered the waters off southern Africa; the boiling sea seethed with man-eating serpents, and the blazing sun turned human flesh black. Some sailors swore that Africa's western shores harbored no life, neither animal nor plant. Others even

A dog-headed Simean, a monster supposedly found in Ethiopia, slays a hapless knight in this 1481 woodcut from a popular European book about Africa. Tales of such fabulous creatures were often accepted as fact by credulous or ignorant Europeans.

repeated the long-disproved theory of a flat earth, fatal to those who ventured beyond its edges.

The sea serpents and boiling oceans were imaginary, of course, but exploration was still fraught with risk. Early-15th-century ships were powered by a combination of winds, currents, tides, and men, none but the tides predictable. A journey could end in disaster when a vessel encountered a tropical storm or when a captain faced a mutinous crew. It could also finish abruptly if a navigator discovered that his maps, the best available at the time, showed him a destination that failed to exist. For each successful journey, countless ships lay on the ocean floor, haunted by sea creatures and forgotten by history.

Portugal, a tiny nation in the southwestern corner of the Iberian Peninsula—itself Europe's most south-

A table illustrates a variety of European navigational methods and instruments used during 17th-century ocean voyages. Even with the best of instruments, a ship's captain usually had to rely on experience and guesswork to determine where his ship was and in which direction it was headed.

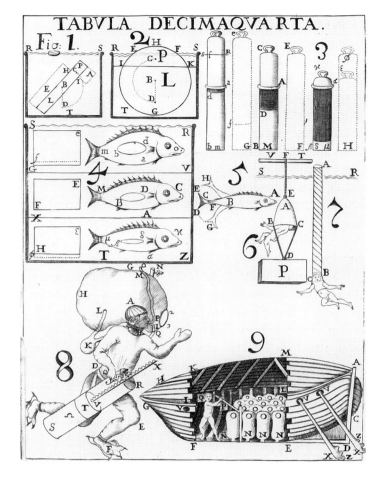

westerly point—gained the first success in exploring the African coast. Chiefly responsible for Portugal's success was Prince Henry (1394–1460), son of the Portuguese king João I and his English wife, Philippa of Lancaster. Gomes Eanes de Zurara, the contemporary chronicler of Portugal's seafaring age, reported that at Henry's birth the stars foretold that "this prince was bound to engage in great and noble conquests, and . . . bound to attempt the discovery of things which were hidden from other men." Indeed, the royal youth, known to history as Henry the Navigator, was to launch the great European Age of Discovery.

Around 1410, King João decided to mount an attack on Ceuta, a Moorish stronghold on the North African side of the Mediterranean. Situated in what is today Morocco, Ceuta guarded the narrowest point of the water—the Strait of Gibraltar—that separated Europe from Africa. The city was an important trade hub for both Mediterranean cargo ships and the camel caravans that snaked in from the East; João wanted a share of this highly profitable commerce. To make the attack even more appealing, Ceuta was controlled by Muslims, and the piously Catholic João knew that the leader of his church, the pope, and the rest of Christian Europe would regard his conquest of the city as worthy and holy.

João put his 21-year-old son, Prince Henry, in charge of the assault on Ceuta, which was launched in 1415. The young prince more than justified his father's faith in him: Ceuta fell in one day. Three years later the Moors attempted to retake Ceuta. Prince Henry led the relief forces, which repelled the Moors, and this time remained in Ceuta for three months. The fleeing Moorish defenders left behind a dazzling trove of colorful silks, gorgeous carpets, spices, ivory, salt, jewels, gold, and silver, all of it brought from the East. From this point on, Henry was determined to reach out for a sea route to the south.

During his stay in Ceuta, Henry interviewed prisoners and merchants and learned a great deal about the commerce and geography of northern Africa. He discovered that Muslim traders regularly crossed the formidable Sahara Desert on well-established trails to trade with the peoples of the "Green Country," a fertile and forested region south of the desert that contains present-day Guinea, Gambia, Senegal, and southern Mali and Niger. Henry learned that the Muslim trad-

ers conducted what was called a silent trade. In this type of commerce, the traders set out a pile of goods, such as salt, cloth, coral beads, and brass utensils. Then they withdrew, and the people of the Green Country came forward and set out a corresponding amount of gold or ivory. Each party then added or subtracted goods until a bargain was struck, all with no contact between the two groups.

Henry found these accounts fascinating, but the Moors and other Muslims controlled the trade routes across the Sahara, effectively closing them to Europeans. Henry soon thought of another possibility: thanks to Portugal's long coastline bordering the Atlantic Ocean, the Portuguese had become experienced and skillful seamen. Henry believed that his nation's sailors and traders could reach the Green Country by sea, bypassing North Africa altogether. He also envisioned reaching the Indies by sailing around the tip of Africa, a far-fetched notion that few of his contemporaries believed possible.

Soon after Henry returned home in 1419, he established an exploration center in Sagres, an Atlantic coast village perched on a cliff at Portugal's southernmost point. To this headquarters, which he stocked with a vast array of charts and books, he invited sailors, sea captains, geographers, mapmakers, travelers, and scholars to come and share their knowledge of the world. From here the enterprising prince oversaw the design and production of new navigational instruments, maps, and seagoing vessels. Of the latter, by far the most important was the caravel, a ship considerably smaller than the huge cargo ships used for centuries in the Mediterranean trade. The caravels were relatively easy to steer, and they rode high in the water, which made them less likely to run aground on

Prince Henry and his colleagues look out to sea from the royal observatory at Sagres. Henry brought together astronomers, cartographers, shipbuilders, and mariners from all over Europe to make a comprehensive study of the science of exploration.

unknown rocky coasts. These little ships were equipped with lateens, curved or triangular sails that enabled them to sail against the wind and that left them less dependent on the prevailing breezes. Ships now traveled faster while using smaller crews.

Out of Sagres, Henry dispatched expeditions to explore the western African coast and its offshore islands. He sent his first ship to the Green Country within a year of returning to Portugal. The ship was blown off course and landed on an island (one of a group now called the Madeiras) to the west of Morocco. When the ship returned, Henry decided to colonize these islands in addition to exploring the African continent itself. Between 1422 and 1434, Henry commissioned 14 voyages, each assigned to find the bottom of Africa and sail around it. Not one of the expeditions accomplished that mission, and Henry soon found himself sharply criticized; he had spent far too much royal money, said his detractors, and achieved far too little.

Then, in 1441, one of Henry's captains returned from the most southerly point yet reached on Africa's coast, bringing with him a new kind of merchandise: 12 slaves. Slave trading had been flourishing in some parts of Africa for centuries, but the return of the Portuguese ship in 1441 marked the beginning of Europe's connection with the capture and sale of black human beings.

When African slaves were first sold at the Portuguese coastal city of Lagos, chronicler Gomes Eanes de Zurara was there. He found the scene strange and moving: "What heart could be so hard as not to be pierced with piteous feeling to see that company?" he wrote. "For some kept their heads low and their faces bathed in tears . . . and it was needful to part father from son,

husbands from wives, brothers from brothers. . . . Mothers would clasp their infants in their arms, and throw themselves on the ground to cover them with their bodies . . . so that they could prevent their children from being separated from them."

European and African traders discuss the purchase of slaves—a scene that became more and more common after the 15th century. Slavery was a well-entrenched practice among Africans, but it differed greatly from the slavery that was practiced in the Americas.

But Zurara, along with Prince Henry, was consoled for the heart-wrenching sight by two considerations: Christianity and money. To these staunch Roman Catholics, the captured black people were heathens whose religious conversion would enable them to enter heaven. He and the prince, notes Zurara, "reflected with great satisfaction upon the salvation of souls that before were lost." The saved souls, of course, could then be sold at a profit.

Realizing that the slave business could save his exploration center, Henry speedily entered the new trade. In 1444, he sent an expedition to Africa's western Sahara Coast, specifically to capture human beings. That voyage ended with the delivery of 235 black people (history reveals nothing further about them), the first of the millions of African men and women who would be bought from their own rulers, carried off in European ships, and resold as slaves.

Henry's prompt espousal of the slave trade reflected the peculiar status of slavery in Portugal during the 15th century. The practice had almost disappeared in Europe after the 5th-century fall of the Roman Empire, but by the 10th century, a small European slave trade developed as merchants sold other Europeans to wealthy North Africans. Slavery was not only profitable but also a means of strengthening Christianity: Catholic church authorities decreed that only non-Christians—Jews and other "unbelievers"—could be sold as slaves.

This regulation led to a revival of slavery in Spain and Portugal during the wars that expelled the Moors; to the Christian Spanish and Portuguese, Muslim captives were unbelievers and therefore enslaveable. (This approach worked both ways: the Moors felt perfectly justified in enslaving "infidel"—non-Muslim—Spanish and Portuguese prisoners of war.) Devout Europeans such as Prince Henry (who observed a lifelong vow of celibacy and routinely wore a hair shirt) actually viewed the enslavement of Muslim captives as a Christian duty. As slaves, the Muslims would be prevented from practicing Islam, would receive Christian religious instruction, and would perhaps convert to Christianity, thus saving their souls from eternal damnation. This philosophy also applied to black Africans who were neither Muslim nor Christian; to Prince Henry and like-minded men, slavery was a blessing in disguise for its victims.

No less crucial to the development of the African slave trade was the long history of slavery in Africa itself. Although conditions varied greatly from place to place, the sub-Saharan slave system differed profoundly from the chattel slavery—wherein slaves were considered property, not people—that would later develop in the Americas. (*Sub-Saharan* refers to the vast African area south of the immense Sahara, a 3.5-million-acre desert stretching southward from the river Nile.) In the sub-Saharan region, slaves (often the people of a nation defeated in war) were ruled by lords to whom they paid tribute (often in the form of labor), but they usually had considerable rights and protections. For example, among the Asante, a western African people who lived in modern-day Ghana, a slave could marry, own property, own another slave, testify in disputes, and inherit his master's property—all rights commonly denied slaves in the Americas.

Martin Delany, a celebrated black American physician and abolitionist who traveled through West Africa in 1859, pointed out that in southern Nigeria slaves could not only easily marry into the family of their masters but could also hold positions of political leadership. Not all slaves had such well-established places in society, however. Captives taken in war were often kept as chattel slaves by wealthy and powerful warlords and chiefs. But although their status was

A Portuguese map from 1519 shows the east coast of Africa, the Arabian Peninsula, and the subcontinent of India. By the 16th century, the Portuguese had discovered a trade route around the southern tip of Africa to India and the rest of Asia. Although much of Portugal's resources would go toward exploiting Asia's riches, the country continued to engage in the African slave trade.

similar to that of American slaves, their numbers were fairly small, and their slave status was rarely extended to their children. Over time, they could hope to attain the status of servants or even gain their freedom.

However much practices of slavery differed, Africans and Europeans shared the underlying concept that there was a class of people who could be traded or given as gifts by others. By the early 16th century, Portuguese slavers had stopped raiding the African coast; instead, they engaged in an orderly trade with African slavers. During the 16th century, the Portuguese transported some 50,000 Africans to Europe, where they worked mainly as domestic servants, farmers, and craftspeople.

Another destination for slaves (and one that would prove more typical of future slaving ventures) was the Portuguese colony of São Tomé, situated on a 372-square-mile island off the west coast of Africa. During the last years of the 15th century, colonists had established large sugarcane plantations on the island. Harvesting sugar is extremely hard work: the cane juice must be processed within a day of the harvest or it will spoil. To assist themselves, the settlers on São Tomé began importing large numbers of slaves from the African mainland; by 1600, the colony had imported 270,000 enslaved workers. By the end of the 19th century, that number would increase more than tenfold.

Prince Henry died in 1460, but efforts to reach the base of Africa continued. Even to the hardy sailors of seafaring Portugal, the continent seemed to extend forever, but at last the explorers made the breakthrough. In 1487, Bartolomeu Dias de Novais departed Portugal and sailed down the African coast with two caravels and a supply ship. Ironically, the perils that blocked the previous explorers actually helped Dias. When he reached the coastline of present-day South Africa, his ships encountered strong gale winds; instead of fighting the storm, he let it carry him out to sea. After about two weeks, he picked up a west wind, which carried the ships east for several days. Finally, Dias ordered his ships to steer north, and the lookouts soon reported land on the horizon.

Dias realized that this new coastline ran not from north to south, as it had during his journey from Portugal, but from west to east. He was situated off Africa's southern coast, which meant that he had reached the goal of all the previous expeditions: the bottom of the African continent. Sure now that the Indies lay ahead, Dias planned to continue, but his crew strongly objected, and he set sail for home. Still, he had sailed 1,260 miles further than any European explorer before him and had opened a new chapter in the relations between his own world and the land long called the Dark Continent.

Ultimately, the attention of the Portuguese focused beyond Africa. In 1499, the explorer Vasco da Gama opened an important new trade route when he became the first person to sail from Portugal around the African continent to the Indian subcontinent and back again. The Portuguese government quickly directed most of the country's maritime resources toward the exploitation of India's and the rest of Asia's wealth of gold and spices. With the Portuguese occupied elsewhere, British, French, and Dutch traders began making inroads on the African trade. Initially these traders neglected slaves, concentrating instead on gold, ivory, and pepper. Indeed, the market for slaves was so poor that when one British expedition brought five Africans to England during the 1540s, no one wanted them. The captives were eventually returned to Africa.

But the slave trade was on the verge of a rapid expansion. Hearing rumors that good money was to be made in this new form of commerce, British pirate John Hawkins decided to try it in 1562. He persuaded a group of London investors to provide him with three ships, then sailed with his men for the west coast of Africa. There they raided Portuguese slaving vessels, carrying off at least 300 African captives. Hawkins then traveled to the Spanish island colony of Hispaniola (site of present-day Haiti and the Dominican Republic) in the Caribbean Sea and traded the prisoners for five shiploads of hides, sugar, spices, and pearls. Spanish authorities seized the ships, but later voyages met with more success and vastly increased Hawkins's fortune.

By the end of the 17th century, Portuguese, British, French, Dutch, Danish, Swedish, and Prussian slave traders along Africa's west coast were engaged in fierce competition that sometimes erupted into open warfare. The traffic in slaves, once a small part of the larger European-African trade, was now the dominant form of commerce. Europeans were even trading gold for slaves—a practice unheard of a century earlier. Triggering this sudden explosion in the slave trade were events taking place half a world away, in the immense territory known as the Americas.

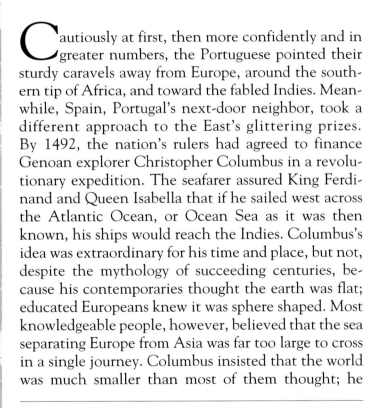

2

THE NEW WORLD

Cautiously at first, then more confidently and in greater numbers, the Portuguese pointed their sturdy caravels away from Europe, around the southern tip of Africa, and toward the fabled Indies. Meanwhile, Spain, Portugal's next-door neighbor, took a different approach to the East's glittering prizes. By 1492, the nation's rulers had agreed to finance Genoan explorer Christopher Columbus in a revolutionary expedition. The seafarer assured King Ferdinand and Queen Isabella that if he sailed west across the Atlantic Ocean, or Ocean Sea as it was then known, his ships would reach the Indies. Columbus's idea was extraordinary for his time and place, but not, despite the mythology of succeeding centuries, because his contemporaries thought the earth was flat; educated Europeans knew it was sphere shaped. Most knowledgeable people, however, believed that the sea separating Europe from Asia was far too large to cross in a single journey. Columbus insisted that the world was much smaller than most of them thought; he

In this romanticized engraving, explorer Christopher Columbus claims the Caribbean island of Hispaniola and its awed occupants for Christianity and for Spain. Although Columbus is often credited with discovering the New World, he was convinced he had reached Asia.

33

persuaded Ferdinand and Isabella that finding a new way to travel to Asia was both possible and potentially very profitable.

Columbus was mistaken about the size of the world, and he did not discover a new route from Europe to India. His reputation as a great explorer rests, in fact, on an accident: his unexpected discovery in 1492 of an enormous land mass between Europe and Asia—the Americas. Columbus realized he and his men were not the first people to set foot in this New World; he encountered local residents as soon as he landed. (He could not have known, however, that these residents—originally natives of Asia—had first reached North America anywhere from 15,000 to 30,000 years before his own arrival.)

Actually, Columbus was not even the first European to reach America, having been beaten to the continent by Viking explorers 500 years earlier. But unlike the Vikings, the Europeans of Columbus's day possessed the navigational technology to cross the seas with regularity and to establish and support settlements. The Vikings' discovery would be forgotten for centuries, but Columbus's would introduce a long and continuing relationship between Europe and the Americas.

Unfortunately for the New World's native inhabitants, this relationship was quickly marred by exploitation and greed. As Columbus was acutely aware, his reputation—perhaps even his life—depended on the profitability of his expedition. Accordingly, he spent much of his first voyage to the Americas (he would ultimately make four) looking for gold on one Caribbean island or another. The islands' inhabitants (named "Indios"—Indians—by Columbus, who mistakenly believed that he had reached the Indies) readily aided their visitors in this quest, directing them toward the island he named Hispaniola. Here, the Europeans found gold in abundance.

Columbus believed that he had also found another resource, one almost as valuable as gold: free labor. The area's inhabitants, Columbus wrote in the log of his first journey, were "fit to be ordered about and made to work, to sow and do aught else that may be needed." He also observed:

> "To rule here, one need only get settled and assert authority over the natives, who will carry out whatever they are ordered to do. I, with my crew—barely a handful of men—could conquer all these islands with no resistance whatsoever. The Indians always run away; they have no arms,

This portrait of Columbus (completed after his death) reflects the steely resolve that enabled him to complete the long and dangerous voyage to the Americas. Columbus and his men proved equally determined to enslave the natives of Hispaniola and extract the island's wealth of gold.

nor the warring spirit. They are naked and defenseless, hence ready to be given orders and put
to work."

But the Native Americans had more "warring spirit" than Columbus thought; when he
returned to Spain, he left a group of settlers on
Hispaniola; when he made his second journey to
the region, he found the settlers slaughtered. But
Columbus never gave up the idea that the people
of the New World should serve the Europeans.
In the late 1490s, he sent 500 Caribbean natives
as a "gift" to Ferdinand and Isabella (who in-
formed him that he was to convert the Indians to
Christianity, not to enslave them). He also instituted a program on Hispaniola whereby each
Native American male over the age of 14 was
required, on pain of death, to produce enough
gold every three months to fill a small flask.

For the Native Americans, Columbus's actions
were merely a taste of things to come. Later Spanish
conquerors such as Hernán Cortés and Francisco
Pizarro found far more gold on the American mainland than Columbus had acquired in Hispaniola. In
addition to this mineral wealth, the climate of the
Americas proved amenable to a number of crops popular in Europe; among them were coffee, sugar, tobacco
(a New World plant that fast gained devotees in
Europe), indigo (a blue dye), and cotton. In order to
exploit the New World's riches, Spain sent conquistadores (men who acted both as explorers and soldiers) to subdue the Native American population and
to organize colonies.

To reward the conquistadores and to encourage settlement, the Spanish government estab-

An engraving from a 1598 German edition of Bartolomé de Las Casas's book History of the Indies *depicts conquistadores maiming and torturing the Native Americans of Florida. Although such wholesale butchery was rare, more ordinary forms of mistreatment were quite common.*

lished the *encomienda* system in the early 1500s. Under the encomienda, loyal Spanish soldiers were allowed to enslave a certain number of Native Americans provided that they supplied their captives with military protection and religious instruction. Opportunities for abuse abounded, and reports of the conquistadores' brutality to the Indians quickly caused the encomienda system to come under scrutiny.

Among the system's most outspoken opponents was Bartolomé de Las Casas, a Dominican priest from Seville, Spain. Born in 1472, Las Casas obtained both religious and military training before joining a 1502 expedition to Hispaniola. There, he was granted an encomienda for his assistance in putting down a Native American uprising, but he gave up the grant when he went to Rome in 1506 to become a priest. Las Casas returned to the Americas in 1512 and served as a chaplain in the Spanish military force that conquered Cuba in 1513, for which service he was granted another encomienda. The next year, Las Casas shocked his contemporaries by renouncing his grant and becoming an ardent crusader against the encomienda system.

It would be 1542 before Las Casas's efforts paid off with the passage of the New Laws of the Indies, which ended the granting of encomiendas. Meanwhile, the priest's first journey back to Spain to plead against the system, which took place in 1515, proved unsuccessful. It also had unintended but dire consequences for millions of Africans. When faced with the question of who would perform the labor being done by Native American slaves, Las Casas recommended replacing the Indians with Europeans or Africans.

Las Casas's suggestion has caused some historians to blame him for the development of African slavery in the Americas, but the idea of transporting slaves to the Americas was not a new one. The Spanish throne had issued its first laws regarding the export of slaves from Spain to the Americas in 1501. Initially, Africans were not seen as candidates; Europeans were considered both more loyal and more likely to be of use in the effort to convert the Native Americans to Christianity. But labor shortages in the colonies made these restrictions unrealistic. Sporadic imports of small groups of African slaves did occur before Las Casas's fateful visit to Spain, the largest consisting of about 200 people.

The labor provided by African slaves at this time was tiny compared to that provided by Native Americans. But Spanish colonists were

already experiencing difficulties with Indian slaves. Indians generally knew the territory better than their Spanish overlords, making escapes and rebellions much harder to prevent. In addition, Native Americans were extremely susceptible to smallpox and other diseases that were common in Europe and Africa but had not previously existed in the Americas. Because the Native Americans had never been exposed to these diseases, they had developed no natural immunities and were much more likely to die from infection than either Europeans or Africans. By the early 16th century, epidemics were rapidly wiping out the Native American popula-

This drawing, made by a member of the Aztec tribe of central Mexico, illustrates the devastation of smallpox, a deadly disease brought to the New World by European settlers. Smallpox and other European diseases ravaged the Native American population, wiping out entire nations.

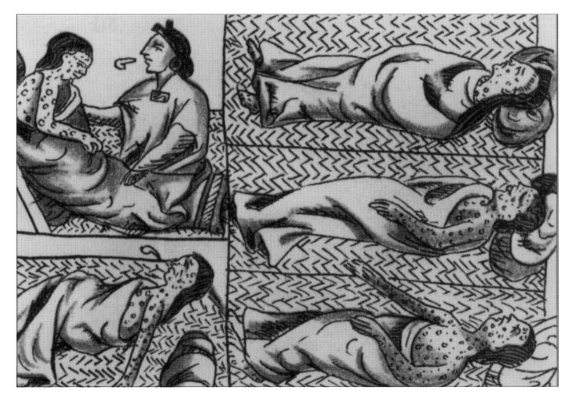

tion in the Caribbean, and colonists and officials began to fear that disease would soon exterminate all the Native Americans on the mainland as well.

The possible annihilation of the Americas' indigenous population presented a disturbing prospect to the Spanish. Some, including Las Casas, felt ardently that such a genocide would be an atrocity. Others were merely concerned about preserving a potentially useful labor force. In any case, due in large part to Las Casas's advocacy, protecting the Native Americans soon became a cornerstone of official Spanish policy in the New World. In keeping with this policy, the Spanish crown placed tight restrictions on the uses of Indian labor, mandating decent working conditions and the payment of wages.

These restrictions were ignored by colonists whenever possible, but their very existence prompted colonists to seek laborers who enjoyed no such protection. They did not have to look for long; in 1518, a mere three years after Las Casas's plea to the throne, the Spanish crown approved the first direct shipment of slaves from Africa to the Americas. This transport was notable not only for the route it followed, but also for its size—4,000 slaves, or almost 20 times the largest previous shipment.

What began as an effort to protect the people of one continent would result in phenomenal suffering for the people of another, but the early-16th-century Europeans seemed untouched by the situation's bitter irony. Colonists enthusiastically reported that one African slave could do the work of four or even eight Native Americans, and not even the relatively enlightened Las Casas renounced his endorsement of African slavery until the late 1540s. A common misconception among Europeans held that Native

Americans were fragile and delicate, whereas Africans were strong, hearty, and uniquely able to withstand backbreaking labor. Consequently, enslaving Africans was considered almost a humane act because Africans were believed capable of surviving work conditions that would kill others.

Modern observers might see such a rationale as an obvious sham, but it was taken quite seriously in its day. One order, given from the king of Spain to his viceregal council in Mexico in 1584, even dictated that "the Indians, a weak people, be left to their own business, and that the labor of the mines, construction, fields and mills be undertaken by mulattoes [people of mixed African and European descent], negroes and mestizos [people of mixed Native American and European descent]."

The attempt to protect the "weak" Native Americans not only helped create African slavery in America but affected its development. For example, the majority of slaves shipped to the Americas came from West Africa partly because the Spanish wished to "protect" the Native Americans from the "infidel" religion of Islam, which was less commonly practiced by Africans south of the Sahara.

> The early and aggressive importation of Africans into the New World meant that many Africans took part in the Spanish drive to expand their American empire. Although their names have for the most part been lost to history, Africans accompanied and sometimes rendered lifesaving assistance to a variety of Spanish explorers and conquerors, including Pizarro in his conquest of the Incas of Peru, Cortés in his conquest of the Aztecs of Mexico, Vasco Nuñez de Balboa in his expedition to the Pacific Ocean,

Hernán Cortés (center) meets with the Aztec emperor Montezuma, whose kingdom he would conquer in 1521. Africans helped make possible the Spanish acquisition of large areas of the New World.

and Francisco Vásquez de Coronado in his conquest of the Pueblo Indians of the American Southwest. Indeed, the American Southwest was opened to Spanish exploration thanks to the leadership of a North African Moor named Estevanillo or Estevanico, who led the first Spanish expedition into the area (and met his death at the hands of hostile Native Americans) in 1539.

The Spanish were handicapped in importing slaves because they had no landholdings in Africa and were prevented from acquiring any under the terms of a 1494 treaty with Portugal. Also hampering Spain in the slave trade was its small and undeveloped maritime shipping industry. Initially, the Spanish crown extended to its colonies a previous agreement that allowed Portugal to ship African slaves to Spain. After 1595, however, Spain began to grant foreign traders permission to ship slaves to its colonies. This permit, known as the *asiento,* was a specific contract between the crown and the slave supplier. The agreement specified the number of slaves to be shipped to the Spanish colonies in America, their places of origin and arrival, and sometimes their price.

In this era, the Spanish crown controlled the slave trade tightly. Only a slaver holding the asiento could legally do business in the Spanish colonies, although a licensed slaver could enlist other traders to provide part of the shipment. Smuggling, too, was a lucrative if dangerous option. With the exception of the slave trade, the Spanish government forbade all commerce between its colonies in the Americas and foreign merchants; consequently, a non-Spanish trader who obtained the asiento had a rare opportunity to smuggle other goods into the Spanish colonial market.

Among traders of various nationalities, competition for the asiento was fierce, and the granting of the license soon took on diplomatic overtones. During the many European wars of the 16th, 17th, and 18th centuries, several countries forced Spain to grant them the asiento in exchange for peace. The asiento provided a tremendous boost to the slave trade, often turning what had been small-scale smuggling operations into large industries. By the 18th century, merchants of nearly every sizable European country (as well as the future United States of America) were engaged in the African slave trade. At the same time, most of these countries had acquired New World colonies, all—with the exception of the Portuguese colony of Brazil—established in defiance of Spain.

A German map drawn in 1540 shows the islands and continents of Die Nüm Welt *(the New World). A pennant has been placed in the Caribbean (center right) to show that these lands are claimed by Spain.*

Helping to topple the mighty Spaniards were members of an unlikely army: Africans who had been brought to the New World in chains. Their masters, logically assuming that forced marches, whips, separation from family, and a seemingly endless sea journey in a reeking, tossing prison had destroyed the Africans' will, must have been astonished by their courage and resourcefulness. Among those who chose to live free or die was a man known only as Diego, a self-emancipated, African-born former slave of the Spanish.

Diego entered the pages of history in 1572, when Francis Drake, an English adventurer (and friend of the first English slaver, John Hawkins), staged a raid on Nombre de Dios (Name of God), a Spanish settlement on the coast of present-day Panama. Seeing the English attack as a God-given opportunity, Diego joined the raiders, then began to help them plan other, more complex attacks on Spain's New World outposts and transport ships. Drake's highly successful assaults (which ultimately sparked a war between England and Spain that decisively weakened Spanish power) were made possible by the aid of Diego and the *cimarrones*, blacks who had escaped slavery to live free in the mountains, where they established their own communities.

At Drake's request, Diego enlisted scores of cimarrones, who were more than ready to join in any move against the hated Spanish. As one of Drake's lieutenants said of them in his journal, they welcomed the chance "to revenge the wrongs and injuries which the Spanish nation had done them." Fearless and quick to learn the ways of European-style sea and land warfare, the Africans proved invaluable allies of the English pirates. The cimarrones were also knowledgeable about local trails and the routes used by the Spanish mule trains that carried plundered treasure to the coast for shipment back to Europe. With their help, Drake not only bedeviled the Spanish but captured fabulous wealth.

The English-cimarron alliance left the Spanish sputtering with rage and terror. Writing to his superiors in Spain, one official in Panama explained why these black volunteers were so much feared: "Being so thoroughly acquainted with the region and so expert in the bush," he said, "the Negroes will show [the English] methods and means to accomplish any evil design they wish to carry out."

Cimarrones, such as this man, were Africans who escaped slavery and established their own communities in the inaccessible mountains of Central America. They provided English pirate Francis Drake with invaluable intelligence and assistance during his attacks on their would-be masters, the Spanish.

Sir Francis Drake (1540–1596), the scourge of the Spanish, appears in this portrait with his hand on the globe, which he successfully circumnavigated in 1580.

Diego and a number of his fellow cimarrones remained with Drake for years, serving as seamen, navigators, soldiers, and scouts. Recognizing Diego's exceptional skills, Drake made him his personal aide, taking the loyal and resourceful cimarron back to England and, later, signing him up for the so-called voyage of the century, a round-the-globe journey that would affect history forever. Drake and his five-ship fleet left England in late 1577; a year later, they were heading north along the western coast of South America. When they reached what is now called Mocha Island off the shore of central Chile, Drake sent a landing party ashore to search for food and fresh water.

Unfortunately, the only Europeans whom the islanders (probably members of the Araucanian tribe) had ever seen were Spanish soldiers, who had made haste to kill and enslave them. The Araucanians attacked at once, killing 13 of the strangers. One of them was Diego, a brave man who had made an immense journey. He had started his voyage from western Africa to western South America as a chained slave; he had ended it as a free man who helped change the shape of the world.

3

RACE SLAVERY

Europeans founded most of their New World colonies for profit. These colonists were more interested in exploiting the Americas' valuable natural resources than in forming permanent settlements. A European who developed a New World gold mine or sugar plantation could return home rich—and many did, never staying long in the Americas. Slavery fit in well with this get-rich-and-get-out approach: free workers would need schools, churches, and other social institutions, all built at their employer's expense. Slaves, on the other hand, needed no such frills. They were relatively inexpensive to buy; they could be cheaply fed, clothed, and housed; they could be worked from sunrise to moonrise.

But many settlers came to North America, especially in the 1600s, not for money but for new homes. Some of these colonists were religious dissidents (rebels against conventional church practices); some were poor farmers and craftspeople who felt the British Isles had little to offer them. They hoped to create

Dutch traders unload slaves at the port of Jamestown, Virginia. African slaves first arrived at the North American colony in 1619, one year before the landing of the Mayflower *at Plymouth Rock, Massachusetts.*

49

their own fresh society on America's shores. Initially at least, these colonists did not engage in large-scale plantation agriculture, and the North American continent did not appear to possess the mineral wealth of the Spanish possessions further south.

The native population of the North American continent was generally hostile and in any case quite small, so the British colonists never had the opportunity to enslave Native Americans in large numbers. Indeed, the area did not encourage the large-scale importation of slaves; only 5 percent of the Africans shipped to the New World wound up in these colonies. Nonetheless, the enslavement of Africans became a common, accepted, and well-entrenched practice in the future United States.

The first African captives to reach the North American colonies arrived in August 1619, a year before the Pilgrims' celebrated Massachusetts landing in the *Mayflower*. These Africans, 20 in all, had already been given Spanish names but were brought on a Dutch ship, giving rise to the speculation that they were taken in a raid on a Spanish slaver (the name of the Dutch ship was never recorded). The ship landed at the settlement of Jamestown, Virginia, where its crew traded the captives for supplies and sailed away again.

The status of these Africans in the new colony is unclear; they may have been considered indentured servants (people who worked without pay for some years and were then granted their freedom) rather than slaves. Certainly many of the Africans who followed them were considered as such. For example, Anthony

Johnson, a black man who arrived in Jamestown from England in the early 1620s, is cited in colonial documents as having worked out his term of indenture, accumulated property, and imported five servants of his own (some of whom were white).

Anthony Johnson and his fellow Africans all came to North America in small shipments that were often transported by pirates from areas other than Africa. During the early 17th century, the British themselves had few commercial contacts in Africa and were barely involved in the slave trade (a situation that would change dramatically after 1650). Hostilities between the British and the Spanish and Portuguese cut off the colonists' access to slaves, except for those seized by Dutch pirates. But the small supply of Africans provided by pirates was usually expensive.

The high price of slaves reflected the chronic labor shortages that plagued the colonies. Land was readily available, and even a relatively poor man could afford to clear and plant farmland and become his own master. But for wealthier colonists, who owned more land and needed people to help work it, getting enough servants was a never-ending problem. Consequently, various forms of forced labor became popular early in the colonies. During the first half of the 17th century, most of their workforce came from England, where work was hard to find and where the poor lived under miserable conditions. These laborers came into the colonies as indentured servants, repaying the person who arranged their transportation by working without pay for a set period of time, usually four to seven years.

By 1625, indentured servants comprised more than 40 percent of Virginia's population; in New England, they made up about 35 percent of the work-

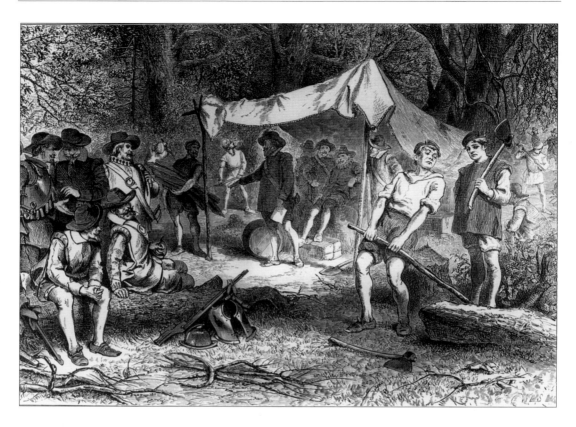

Servants do heavy labor while richly dressed lords look on near the settlement at Jamestown. Indentured servants were usually recruited from the poorest classes in England and often deeply resented the wealth of their masters.

force. Cheaper than African slaves and more tractable than Native American laborers, these indentured servants nevertheless presented their employers with certain problems. For one thing, they were expensive to import, and if they proved unsatisfactory, their masters were out the cost of their transportation from England.

Another problem arose when indentured servants became free. Most were uneducated men between the ages of 15 and 24, and they did not always find it easy to make a living or to blend into colonial society. This fact was dramatically underscored in Virginia in 1676 when Nathaniel

Nathaniel Bacon (right center) and Sir William Berkeley quarrel on the streets of Jamestown as a gun-toting mob looks on. "How miserable that man is," Berkeley complained on the eve of the rebellion, "that Governes a People where six parts of seaven at least are Poor Endebted Discontented and Armed."

Bacon, a young, wealthy newcomer from England, led an uprising of colonists (many of them former indentured servants) against both the local Native Americans and the colonial governor, Sir William Berkeley. The rebels drove

Berkeley out of Jamestown twice, burning down the town during the second attack. Berkeley did not regain control of the colony until the end of the year, and he might not have done so at all had Bacon not died from a fever. Virginia's governing officials blamed Bacon's Rebellion, as the uprising was known, on the large number of poor and dissatisfied former servants in the colony. In response, the state began to encourage the importation of African slaves instead of English indentured servants. This new policy coincided with an increase in Britain's involvement in the slave trade, which had grown tremendously in order to provide laborers for the booming sugar plantations in the British Caribbean colonies. Africans were now more available than ever, and by the end of the century, Virginia had imported some 10,000 slaves.

The original reasons for using African slaves were economic and social, but other rationales, many of them religious in nature, also came into play. In 1706, Cotton Mather, a respected leader among the Puritans (a sect of Protestant Christians centered in New England), published a work entitled *The Negro Christianized*. Much as Prince Henry of Portugal had done, Mather defended the enslavement of "heathen" Africans and Native Americans as a sacred privilege, granted by God to his chosen Puritans. Many colonists believed that slavery was condoned in the Bible and that the scriptures were quite specific as to who could be enslaved. The colonists translated these ideas into their legal codes. A 1641 Massachusetts statute, for example, declares:

> There shall never be any bond slaverie, villinage or Captivitie amongst us, unless it be lawfull Captives taken in

just warres, and such strangers as willingly sell themselves or are sold to us. And these shall have all the liberties and Christian usages which the law of God established in Israell concerning such persons doth morally require. This exempts none from servitude who shall be Judged thereto by Authoritie.

Initially, these rules were strictly followed, and those who broke them were punished under a Massachusetts law that stated in part "he that stealeth a man, and selleth him . . . shall surely be put to death." In 1645, for example, colonial authorities arrested two Massachusetts slave merchants and returned their captives to Africa because the traders had raided an African town for the sole purpose of kidnapping slaves. Taking captives in this manner was considered stealing rather than slave trading (although the death penalty was apparently not applied in this case). But as New

On the shores of Chesapeake Bay, African slaves pack and load barrels of tobacco while merchants and sailors take inventory and chat. By 1750, the date of this illustration, more than 100,000 slaves had been imported into the American South.

New England Puritans thank God for the safe arrival of a supply ship to their colony. An extremely religious people, the Puritans justified slavery as an appropriate lot for nonbelievers.

Englanders became more involved in the slave trade, it became abundantly clear that the "strangers [who] are sold to us" were often obtained through measures that qualified as man stealing. There was such a fine line between the stealing of men and the trading of slaves that New England soon abandoned the legal distinction. The 1645 case is the last recorded instance of slave traders being so prosecuted.

The 1641 Massachusetts statute not only regulated the taking of captives. It also contained one of the few clauses in British colonial law aimed at protecting the rights of slaves. They shall, said the regulation, "have all the liberties and Christian usages which the law of God established in Israell concerning such persons doth morally require." But legal codes concerning slaves' rights in the British colonies were usually composed by slaveholders. Predictably enough, they concentrated on restricting slaves' movements and actions in order to lessen the chance of rebellion. The few passages outlining slaves' rights were (like the above statute) hopelessly vague. As a result, the United States would eventually consider slaves as property rather than as people, with no more rights or privileges than livestock or furniture—a concept unknown in other nations' New World colonies.

Other characteristics that would distinguish slavery in the United States developed as the institution became more common in the latter half of the 17th century. Christian colonists had at first defended slavery as an appropriate fate for nonbelievers, but increasing numbers of Africans were converting to Christianity or were already converted when they arrived. To preserve slavery, Virginia passed a law in 1667 stating that "the conferring of [Christian] baptisme doth not alter the condition of the person as to his bondage or freedom," and other colonies quickly followed suit. Eventually, those who "deserved" slavery came to be identified by a new means: race. Laws began to define slaves not as heathens but as "Negroes" or "blacks," often using the words *slave, Negro,* and *black* interchangeably. Likewise, the word *free* became a synonym for *English* and later (as more Europeans arrived from countries other than England) for *white.*

Colonial authorities did their best to keep the races "pure," that is, segregated. But in one sense, their job was done for them; the colonies were naturally segregated. Accounting for this phenomenon were British immigration patterns. The settlers, who expected to remain in their new homes forever, usually brought their families with them; indeed, entire English villages sometimes relocated in America. The result was a relatively equal male-female ratio, allowing ample opportunity for white Britons to marry each other and little temptation to look for mates of another race.

By contrast, in many of the Central and South American colonies, the European—usually Spanish or Portuguese—population was overwhelmingly male; the military and commercial organizations that had sent them to the New World excluded women. Because same-race women were in such short supply, the male Europeans in these colonies were much more likely to marry women of African or Native American descent and raise mixed-race children. The result was a large multiracial population. By 1800 for example, the population of the Spanish colony of New Granada (encompassing modern-day Panama, Colombia, Venezuela, and Ecuador) was fully 50 percent mulatto. As a result, these southern societies were far more flexible about racial distinctions than their North American counterparts.

While interracial marriages occurred everywhere in the New World, the North American British colonial authorities did everything possible to discourage them. In 1664, the colony of Maryland adopted the first antimiscegenation (against interracial coupling) statute. Its preamble reads in part:

> And forasmuch as divers freeborn *English* women, forgetful of their free condition, and to the disgrace of our nation, do intermarry with Negro slaves, . . . for preservation whereof for deterring such free-born women from such shameful matches, *be it enacted:* That whatsoever free-born woman shall intermarry with any slave . . . shall serve the master of such slave during the life of her husband; and

that all the issue [children] of such free-born women, so
married, shall be slaves as their fathers were.

Virginia followed suit in 1691 with an equally harsh
law, this one dictating banishment for any "white
man or woman being free who shall intermarry
with a negro, mulatto, or Indian man or woman bond
or free," and by 1717 similar statutes existed in Massachusetts, North Carolina, South Carolina, and
Delaware.

Such laws had a number of effects, all of them
disadvantageous to African slaves. They cut off one
avenue to freedom for slaves and their descendants.
They explicitly set off whites as being inherently
better and more deserving of freedom than blacks.
And they pointedly discouraged whites from having
equitable and legitimate social and sexual relationships with blacks. Race slavery not only had lasting
effects on the way American blacks and whites per-
ceived each other and themselves: according to historian Basil Davidson in his 1961 book *Black Mother:
The Years of the African Slave Trade*, "slaving also
became, as a matter of fact or a matter of myth, the
great conditioning factor of most European ideas
about Africa; and this is where myth and fact about
Africans have become most confounded."

4

THE SLAVE TRADE
IN AFRICA

The precise number of Africans captured and delivered to the New World will probably never be known. Most historians estimate the figure at 10 to 20 million, but slavers may have captured two or three times as many Africans; a high percentage of captives died on their way to the Americas.

The slave trade did not affect all areas of Africa in the same way. Some peoples saw their population decimated; others suffered minor losses but were deeply involved as traders; and still others were little affected. In addition, different areas of Africa were more involved in the trade at certain times than at others.

The slave trade was most heavily concentrated along the west coast of Africa, extending from Cape Verde in present-day Senegal to the region of modern Angola. During the 18th and 19th centuries, the trade gradually shifted to the more southern portions of this area, with the southernmost Angola-Congo area sharply increasing its share of the trade during the 19th century. In addition to the trade in West Africa,

An enslaved man grimly awaits his fate on the bank of a river in what is now Zaire (formerly the Belgian Congo). Between 1800 and 1850, more than 7 million slaves were exported from the Congo River Basin area alone.

Portuguese traders also slaved heavily along the east coast. The East African trade has been less well researched and figures are for the most part unavailable, but it is estimated that during the period from 1817 to 1843 alone, 116,000 slaves were shipped into Brazil from present-day Mozambique and Madagascar.

But few slaves came from the area where they were sold; Africans who traded with Europeans in the coastal areas rarely sold their own citizens into slavery. Instead, coastal peoples usually sold slaves purchased from the interior; thus most of the African slaves shipped to the Americas came from areas several hundred miles inland. The coastal peoples had the advantage of not being exploited for slaves as well as having the first pick of the European goods exchanged in the trade. Furthermore, because of their location, people on the coast could fairly easily prevent European traders from directly contacting the people of the heartland. The coastal Africans played this middle-man role for all it was worth, successfully repelling a number of European attempts to gain personal access to central Africa.

The coastal peoples were less successful at repelling powerful interior nations that decided to make their own deals with the Europeans. During the years of the slave trade, the empires of Benin, Dahomey, and Asante spread to include shoreline territory, expansions that were made easier when the European traders introduced firearms to Africa. Guns also greatly facilitated the growth of the slave trade, because those who had them could easily conquer and enslave those without them. When unarmed Africans tried to obtain weapons from Europeans, they discovered that these traders would accept only slaves in exchange. This greatly increased the slave trade's intensity. Africans who had once only dabbled in the

A European slave trader haggles with his African counterpart while inspecting a captive. Coastal Africans often acted as middlemen between the Europeans and the peoples of the African interior.

business of selling human beings found themselves dependent upon it for defense and even survival.

Although the Europeans profoundly influenced African society during the slave-trade period, they never commanded much actual power in Africa and, with the exception of the Portuguese, made few inroads into the continent. Western peoples of the 19th and 20th centuries have often averred that the Africans had no highly developed culture or sophisticated political structures before the Europeans arrived in the 15th century; European slave traders would have strongly disagreed. The Africans who provided the slavers with captives boasted complex customs, societies, and economies; a European trader who violated local traditions, slighted a powerful trade official, or failed to provide his African counterparts with the desired goods might return from the continent empty-handed. Further complicating matters was a wide variety from place to place in customs, political structures, and market demands.

But all African traditions and economies had one thing in common: they bore little resemblance to those of the Europeans, and the slave trade was almost always accomplished in the face of mutual misunderstanding. One fundamental difference between Europeans and Africans of this era was their means of measuring wealth. Europeans judged an individual's financial importance by the amount of money and property he or she owned. In contrast, Africans usually measured wealth in terms of political power, or by the number of people who were loyal to and dependent upon a particular individual. Instead of developing European banking systems, Africans developed sophisticated systems of patronage; instead of stockpiling riches, they distributed them in order to increase their followers.

This difference in calculating wealth confused the Europeans. For example, cloth was a popular trade item, but Africans would deal with it only by the "piece," a bolt of material about six feet long. An African slave trader would not bargain for sections of a piece, but only for whole pieces, whereas the Europeans were accustomed to selling cloth in various units of feet and inches. To the Africans, however, a whole bolt of cloth was needed to dress a person, and clothing—especially that made of rare, foreign cloth—was a valuable gift that could secure loyalty among dependents. A fragment of a piece could dress no one and was therefore worthless to an African seeking wealth as his culture defined it.

The Africans' refusal to deal in fragments of cloth brought about the development of the "bundle," a peculiar—and to the Europeans, most inconvenient—form of currency. A bundle was a standard package of trade goods considered to be of equal value to one healthy male slave. In time, these assortments of objects (many of them from different European countries and colonies) became fixed and sometimes remarkably complex. For example, records kept by slave traders show one transaction in which a young woman was exchanged for one roll of tobacco, 24 linen handkerchiefs, one gun, one jug, four pint mugs, and three lengths of cloth. In another transaction, a man and a female child were exchanged for a roll of tobacco, a string of coral beads, one gun, three cutlasses, one blunderbuss (a type of firearm), 25 linen handkerchiefs, five fabric patches, three jugs of rum, 12 pewter utensils, 12 pint mugs, and one lace hat. If a bundle lacked even one expected item, the Africans would refuse to trade slaves for it.

Delays were common in the trading process, and gathering enough captives to fill a ship often took several months. Highly susceptible to common tropical diseases (especially yellow fever and malaria), Europeans dreaded these holdups. Those visiting Africa often suffered mortality rates of 50 percent, and the longer a ship stayed in the area, the more likely its crew was to die of disease. Delays also increased the chances of epidemics among the imprisoned slaves; European slavers sometimes lost an entire shipload of captives before even leaving Africa.

To decrease the spread of disease, slavers anchored their ships away from the land and tried to go ashore as seldom as possible. If a ship's captain was very lucky, African slavers would have a large number of captives already assembled for purchase. But more commonly, African slave dealers on the coast preferred to go inland and obtain captives only when they knew a buyer was available. Consequently, the Europeans had to forward payment for the slaves to their African

African slave merchants (center, in hats) confer with European slavers at a 19th-century West African port. Meanwhile, sailors prepare their captured "merchandise" for shipment across the Atlantic.

counterparts, then wait for their cargo to arrive. The African middleman usually left a hostage, often a close relative, with the Europeans; this individual would be taken into bondage if the African trader failed to deliver. But to the Europeans, a single hostage was no replacement for a full cargo of slaves, and there was always the risk that actually carrying off the hostage would offend the local leaders, thereby crippling future trade in the area.

Another way to minimize time spent ashore was to maintain a European, called a factor, at every important slave-trading port. In theory, the factor would purchase slaves between scheduled ship dockings, so that when the slave ship arrived, the crew could just load the captives aboard and sail away. But factors rarely had an easy time of it. The coastal kingdoms that dealt in slaves tended to be well organized, strong, and not at all eager to have strange Europeans wandering freely about their ports. Consequently, government officials often put limits on whom a factor could see and where he could go, severely hampering his ability to purchase and hold slaves. In the Niger Delta, for example, local authorities would not allow the factors to live on land, restricting them to boats anchored off shore. To add to their difficulties, factors were just as vulnerable to disease as any sailor.

Factors also had to deal with competition from other Europeans. During the centuries of the slave trade, the nations of Europe engaged in numerous clashes. A lone factor in Africa was extremely vulnerable to attack by the ships of rival nations. Trying to shield their factors from such assaults, slaving companies built coastal forts, but these small, makeshift buildings offered little protection from sea- or land-based attacks. In 1694, the slave ship *Hannibal* called at Whydah, a major slave port in Benin. On board was Thomas Phillips, who visited the British Royal African Company's fort, noting in his journal that it stood

The sun shines on the ramparts of Elmina Castle, located in present-day Ghana. Despite its impressive fortifications, the European outpost was repeatedly overpowered by African troops.

> low near the marshes, which renders it a very unhealthy place to live in; the white men the [Royal African] company send there, seldom returning to tell their tale; 'tis compass'd round with a mud wall, about six foot high, and on the south-side is the gate; within is a large yard, a mud thatch'd house, where the factor lives . . . ; also a storehouse, [stocks] for slaves, and a place where they bury their dead white men, call'd, very improperly, the hog-yard.

Forts, whose security depended on the good will of the local Africans, were usually built only after extensive negotiations with coastal authorities. But even the larger forts, such as Elmina on the Gold Coast, were repeatedly overrun by hostile Africans. These attacks were often triggered by Europeans whose countries were at the moment warring with whatever nation occupied the fort.

Because of this vulnerability, a self-interested European slaver behaved with great care, entertaining local officials, distributing gifts, and cheerfully paying high customs fees. Although some African rulers opposed the export of slaves, most cooperated with the traders because it was extremely profitable. Indeed, when the monarch of the Congo empire, the Mani-Congo Nzinga Mbemba (baptized into the Catholic faith by Portuguese missionaries as Dom Affonso), attempted to end the slave trade in 1526, he was defied by his own nobles, who eventually seized much of his power.

> **African slave merchants obtained their captives in a variety of ways. They sometimes simply waylaid and kidnapped them, but this was not an efficient means of obtaining large numbers of people. Prisoners of war were considered enslaveable, but waging wars to get them was highly expensive. Many rulers sold off their own potential troublemakers: criminals, disobedient slaves, or refugees from areas of famine. But the most reliable way to obtain slaves in quantity was to attack weaker peoples.**

Slave raids against neighbors, however, tended to become more costly with time. Frequently assaulted peoples eventually declined in numbers or moved to less accessible areas, forcing the raiders to send battle parties farther and farther inland. In order to move their human merchandise to the point of sale, slavers organized them into coffles and marched them to the coast. British explorer Mungo Park, who traveled extensively through West Africa in the later 18th and

early 19th centuries, described a slave coffle in his 1799 book, *Travels in the Interior Districts of Africa:*

> [Slaves] are commonly secured by putting the right leg of one and the left of another into the same pair of fetters. By supporting the fetters with a string, they can walk, though very slowly. Every four slaves are likewise fastened together by the necks with a strong rope or twisted thongs; and in the night an additional pair of fetters is put on their hands, and sometimes a light iron chain passed round their necks.
>
> Such of them as [show] marks of discontent, are secured in a different manner. A thick billet [piece] of wood is cut about three feet long, and a smooth notch being made upon one side of it, the ankle of the slave is bolted to the smooth part by means of a strong iron staple, one prong of which passes on each side of the ankle.

The billet's purpose was to discourage escape attempts, but such restraints also made the forced march to the coast much more exhausting. Slavers usually fettered their captives at once, freeing them only when they approached their destination—often a distance of several hundred miles from the starting point.

Congolese soldiers rest by the riverside in this woodcut. Despite the opposition of the country's ruler to the slave trade, other nobles continued the traffic in humans, and millions of Congolese people were sold into slavery.

Drivers beat their captives as they march them to a coastal slave port. It is estimated that fully half the captives in an average slave coffle died before reaching their destination.

The traders were also careless about feeding their coffled prisoners, who commonly suffered from malnutrition, which, combined with exhaustion and close quarters, resulted in widespread disease. Slavers whipped captives who were too sick or weak to keep up with the group; if a prisoner failed to respond properly, the slavers simply killed him or her, leaving the body to be eaten by wild animals. Commonly used coffle routes were strewn with human bones.

Not all slave captures resulted from military action: rulers sometimes changed laws and regulations to promote enslavement. An emperor might demand that dependent states pay their regular taxes in slaves or decree that various offenses were to be punished by enslavement and

sale to the Europeans. Such policies not only provided a constant supply of slaves but helped concentrate a ruler's power; his potential rivals could always be enslaved and sold away.

In areas where criminals and debtors were commonly enslaved, they were rarely moved to the coast in coffles. Each of these communities had its own native slaver, a resident who belonged to a regional network of traders. After the courts condemned a man (or woman) to enslavement, they handed him over to this slaver who, in turn, passed him along until he reached the coast and the European buyers. For the slaves, such journeys were physically less draining than those made as part of a coffle; these trips allowed at least minimum rest periods as the prisoners went from one slaver to the next.

Slave traders belonging to the same network often considered themselves kin, even if they were not actually related by blood. But they were no relatives to the communities where they worked. Often of a different ethnic group or religion than their neighbors, they were almost automatically suspect. Even when they worked among their own people, slave traders were often set off from the larger society. In the Congo empire, for example, a would-be trader had to join a cult, known as the *lemba*, before he was allowed to work with the network. Fellow Congolese distrusted lemba members, whom they viewed as hostile sorcerers.

But the social position of the trader was of no significance to the men and women he traded. Whether they had been kidnapped, captured during war, or condemned for bad debts, the millions of Africans sold to the Europeans would never see their homes again. By the time they reached the coastal ports and the slave ships, their lives—and the lives of their descendants—had changed forever.

5

THE MIDDLE PASSAGE

M arched to the coast and loaded onto slave ships, captured Africans next had to face an even worse ordeal: the Middle Passage, the long and painful journey across the Atlantic Ocean to the Americas. The voyage usually lasted two to three months, but bad weather and unexpected currents could make it even longer. For the Africans, the trip was a passage through hell; lucky vessels made it with few casualties, but on the average slave ship, between 20 and 30 percent of the captives died.

Before loading their prisoners aboard, slavers stripped and shaved them (to minimize lice and fleas), then branded them on the shoulder or chest with a red-hot iron (to ensure their permanent identification). At sea, they grouped the male slaves into pairs and chained them together, sometimes so closely that neither man could move without the other. This practice naturally increased the spread of disease. Children and women were not thought to pose a threat, so slavers generally left them unfettered. They

Naked and emaciated, African captives crowd the deck of the 19th-century slave ship Wildfire, *which carried 510 slaves on this 1860 journey. The cramped and squalid conditions of the ships made the lengthy Atlantic crossing a horrifying and sometimes fatal experience.*

This elaborately engraved and cruelly spiked neck collar is only one of the many devices that were used by slave traders (and owners) to restrain and punish their captives.

kept male and female captives strictly segregated, but they did not extend this rule to themselves; both officers and crew usually considered the rape of a female slave acceptable behavior.

If the ocean crossing was fairly short and the ship's captain had bought supplies wisely, the Africans received adequate food and water. Slavers fed them twice or sometimes three times a day with beans, corn, wheat, yams, or rice boiled with fat or oil. (The sale of such provisions to slavers was another source of profit for African merchants.) To prevent scurvy (now known to be a disease brought on by the absence of ascorbic acid in the diet), the crew occasionally gave the slaves lemon juice or vinegar, and they sometimes provided pipes and tobacco as well. If a ship's captain was willing, the crew fed the Africans on deck—possibly the most appetizing aspect of the meal, because the alternative was the hold, where conditions were practically unbearable.

On a large, "loose-pack" ship, captives were arranged on wooden racks below deck. As each individual was allotted a space measuring about

six feet long and one foot wide, the racks allowed their occupants to lie down on their backs. But if the captain was a "tight packer"—one determined to cram in as many captives as possible—slaves would have to lie on their sides, cupped against one another like spoons, or sit between each other's legs and lie back on top of each other. Slavers did not like to waste cargo space on ventilators; as a result, air in the hold was often so foul that candles would not stay lit there. To keep the ship from swamping during storms, the crew blocked off whatever air openings there were, and captives sometimes smothered before the weather cleared.

In these close, unsanitary quarters, a variety of diseases, including smallpox, measles, and dysentery, could spread with appalling speed. Slavers on a relatively well-run ship cleaned out the hold every day and attempted to clear the air with containers of heated vinegar, but other slavers did not bother. Crews on passing vessels often reported that they could smell a slave ship miles away.

Many contemporary observers described slave holds, but Olaudah Equiano, who was born in Benin (now part of Nigeria) in 1745 and was captured as an 11-year-old boy, gave a firsthand account in his autobiography. *The Interesting Narrative of the Life of Olaudah Equiano, or Gustavus Vassa the African, Written by Himself* was published in 1789, several years after the author's emancipation. According to Equiano,

The closeness of the place, and the heat of the climate, added to the number in the ship, which was so crowded

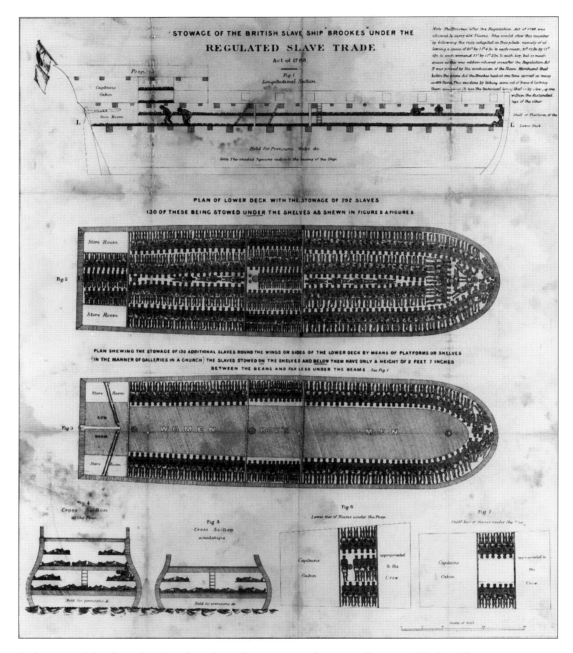

A diagram of the slave ship Brookes *shows how captives fit onto a "loose-pack" ship. Slaves on a "tight-pack" ship did not even have enough room to lie on their backs; instead, slavers forced them to lie on their sides or to sit on one another for the entire eight-week voyage across the Atlantic.*

> that each had scarcely room to turn himself, almost suffocated us. This produced copious perspirations, so that the air soon became unfit for respiration, from a variety of loathsome smells, and brought on a sickness among the slaves, of which many died. . . . This wretched situation was again aggravated by the galling [painful rubbing] of the chains, now become insupportable, and the filth of the necessary tubs [for urine and feces], into which the children often fell, and were almost suffocated. The shrieks of the women, and the groans of the dying, rendered the whole a scene of horror almost inconceivable.

Not surprisingly, captives in the hold would sometimes turn on one another, trying—often successfully—to inflict injury with their chains. Tribal hostility played a large part in these battles; because slavers had no interest in African society, they often shackled together men from tribes that had hated each other for centuries. Trapped in a hellish pit with their worst enemies, these men predictably lashed out in pain and rage.

Conditions became even worse when a trip went badly. If a shortsighted captain had decided to pack fewer supplies and more captives, if the ship was becalmed or blown off course, or if there was a serious outbreak of disease, death rates skyrocketed among captives and crew alike. Indeed, one of the little-known facts about the Middle Passage is that on slave ships, the death rates for sailors averaged about twice that of captives. Partly accounting for this huge difference was European susceptibility to the tropical diseases carried by the Africans. Mortality among the sailors was also increased by floggings and other punishments, at that time a standard element of maritime life.

Physically, then, the slaves' journey was horrifying; psychologically, it may have been even worse.

Starving East Africans rest after being taken from a captured slave ship. Because crew members were rarely willing to go hungry in order to spare their captives, conditions on board became even worse if food rations ran short.

Few of the captured Africans had ever seen the ocean, large sailing ships, or white people; being snatched from familiar terrain and placed in such a strange environment was terrifying. Many prisoners believed their captors were monsters or cannibals. When Equiano first arrived on the ship that took him to America, he recalled,

> I was . . . persuaded that I had gotten into a world of bad spirits, and that they were going to kill me. Their complexions too, differing so much from ours, their long hair, and the language they spoke, which was very different from any I had ever heard, united to confirm me in this belief.

Equiano's countrymen eventually convinced him that the slavers were human beings; but, he said,

> still I feared I should be put to death, the white people looked and acted, as I thought, in so savage a manner; for

I had never seen among any people such instances of brutal
cruelty: and this not only shewn towards us blacks, but also
to some of the whites themselves.

Equiano was not alone in his dread of the whites.
One of the few successful slave revolts at sea, the 1839
mutiny on the *Amistad*, began when the ship's cook,
intending to play a cruel joke, told a captive that he
and the other Africans were to be cut up and eaten by
the whites. Unfortunately for the would-be comedian,
the captive—a brave and intelligent man named
Sing-Gbe (also known as Cinque)—believed him.
After quietly palming a lock pick, he organized an
uprising that resulted in freedom for the captives and
death for the ship's captain and the cook.

More often than not, the result of such panics was
tragedy. One slaver, Captain Japhet Bird of the *Prince
of Orange*, wrote in a 1737 letter that when his ship
docked at the Caribbean island of St. Christopher, "to
our great Amazement above an hundred Men Slaves
jump'd over board" and 33 of them drowned. This
mass suicide occurred, said the slaver, because "one of
their Countrymen [who had been enslaved earlier]
came on board and in a joking manner told the Slaves
that they were first to have their Eyes put out, and
then to be eaten, with a great many other nonsensical
Falsities."

The captives on the *Prince of Orange* were not
alone; accounts of the Middle Passage are filled with
suicides, attempted suicides, and slavers' strategies to
prevent them. Crews watched their captives closely
when they allowed them on deck, punishing those
who tried to jump overboard. To increase security,
sailors hung nets above the rails, and they kept small
boats ready to pursue anyone who evaded the nets.
Some slavers carefully pared the captives' fingernails
to keep them from clawing at each other or themselves; at least one slave was known to have torn open
his own throat with his nails.

A black and a white slave driver lash two defenseless slaves. Whippings, beatings, rape, and other abuses were appallingly common on board slave ships.

Some captives secreted bits of rope and hanged themselves, while others choked themselves with their chains. Especially despondent captives would sometimes die for no discernible reason; these deaths greatly perplexed the slavers, who wondered if some unknown African malady was afoot. Some Africans believed that a person's soul traveled back to its homeland after death, but that if the body was missing a limb, its soul could not make the journey; to discourage suicides, slavers sometimes dismembered the bodies of dead slaves in front of their fellow prisoners. More direct forms of rebellion were common as well. The one most dreaded by slavers was a general uprising, or mutiny. Because the holds were so crowded and filthy, slave-ship crews found it difficult to inspect them carefully, and captives could easily hide lock picks, heavy objects, or makeshift weapons (in one instance, a group of captives brained a slaver with their food bowls).

> **Reports by slavers describe 55 organized revolts during the years of the African slave trade, but many more probably took place and went unrecorded. Despite their frequency, however, these rebellions rarely succeeded. Bowls and makeshift knives were no match for firearms, and slavers cultivated informers who would betray their fellow captives in exchange for special treatment. And even if the prisoners managed to kill the crew, most had no idea how to handle a ship and would simply drift until they died of thirst or hunger.**

Hunger strikes, motivated either by despair or a spirit of protest, were extremely common, and captives who refused to eat were routinely beaten. If the defiance continued, crew members force-fed the slaves, applying hot coals to their lips to force their mouths open and striking them on the throat to induce swallowing. A 1682 travel article by slaver John Barbot proclaimed, "Tho' I must say I am naturally compassionate, yet have I been necessitated sometimes to cause the teeth of those wretches to be broken, because they would not open their mouths, or be prevailed upon by any intreaties to feed themselves; and thus have forced some sustenance into their throats."

In order to maintain their captives' health, slavers sometimes instituted exercise programs and provided medical care, but their tactics were often brutal and degrading. To make the captives' exercises more entertaining for the crew, slavers forced their prisoners

Africans mutiny on an 18th-century slave ship. As one former slaver wrote, "An attempt to rise upon the ship's company, brings on instantaneous and horrid war: for, when [the slaves] are once in motion, they are desperate; and where they do not conquer, they are seldom quelled without much mischief and bloodshed on both sides."

to dance, either to the music of African instruments played by fellow captives or to tunes played by the sailors on bagpipes and fiddles. Crew members usually separated sick captives from the others, allowing them to remain unfettered and to go on deck more often. But if a captain was concerned about disease spreading to the rest of the slaves, he might simply order the sick person thrown overboard. Slavers bathed captives' wounds (often received during flogging) in salt water or vinegar or rubbed them with gunpowder to prevent infection. But even the best European medicine was primitive and often only worsened any sickness. For example, Portuguese slavers treated ailing slaves by feeding them lead, a metal that European doctors did not realize was poisonous.

A cargo of dead slaves, of course, had no value on the market, and sick or crippled slaves had to be sold at a loss. Slavers were thus put in the peculiar position of nursing and caring for the same people they were imprisoning and beating. This combination of care and abuse comes through in slaver Thomas Phillips's account of the 1693–94 crossing of the slave ship *Hannibal:*

> What the small-pox spar'd, the flux [dysentery] swept off, to our great regret, after all our pains and care to give them their messes [meals] in due order and season, keeping their lodgings as clean and sweet as possible, and enduring so much misery and stench so long among a parcel of creatures nastier than swine; and after all our expectations to be defeated by their mortality.

Apologists for the slave trade often claimed that slavers did their very best to keep their captives alive and healthy in order to make a good profit. But financial interest did not always promote the survival of the captive Africans. The investors who financed the journey usually hired a slave ship's captain and crew, and although they received more money if the captives arrived alive, slavers were generally guaranteed a certain salary no matter what happened. In addition, many sailors and captains used the journey as an opportunity to conduct trade of their own on the side; consequently, individual crew members could make money even if they lost most of their slave cargo.

> In some cases, the profit motive and the captives' survival were directly opposed. For example, in 1781 the British slave ship *Zong* was ravaged by disease during the Atlantic crossing. As the vessel neared Jamaica, Captain Luke Collingwood realized that many of the captives either would not make it alive or would command very low prices because of their weakened condition. The slaving venture had been insured (a standard practice at the time), and according to the terms of the insurance, if the slaves died from

Slavers toss captives overboard to certain death. Slave traders routinely jettisoned sick or dead captives; as a result, packs of hungry sharks often followed slave ships along the entire route from Africa to the Americas.

disease or fetched a low price, the *Zong*'s owners would be financially liable. If, however, the slaves were jettisoned overboard alive (to prevent the spread of disease, for example), the insurers would reimburse the owners, and Collingwood would be paid and probably hired again. With this no doubt in mind, the captain picked out 133 of the sickest slaves, fettered them, and threw them overboard in full view of land. But the insurers refused to pay for the murdered captives, and the resulting court case (which was well-publicized due to the efforts of the former captive Olaudah Equiano, who was by then living in London and prospering in business) helped turn British public opinion against the slave trade. The law never charged Collingwood and his men with any wrongdoing.

Among slave traders, disregard for human life was probably more the norm than the exception. John Newton, an 18th-century slaver who underwent a religious awakening and eventually became an ardent opponent of the trade, pointed out that insensitivity to suffering and death was inseparable from the slave trade itself. In his 1788 pamphlet, *Thoughts upon the African Slave Trade*, Newton observed:

> There is a second [evil inherent in the trade], which either is, or ought to be, deemed of importance, considered in a political light: I mean, the dreadful effects of this trade upon the minds of those who are engaged in it. There are, doubtless, exceptions; and I would willingly except myself. But in general, I know no method of getting money, not even that of robbing for it upon the highway, which has so direct a tendency to efface [erase] the moral sense, to rob the heart of every gentle and human disposition, and to harden it, like steel, against all impressions of sensibility.

6

ARRIVAL

Living through the Middle Passage was no guarantee of continued survival. Even the European explorers, merchants, and colonists, who came to the Americas by choice, knew the move was a gamble: they might strike it rich, or they might succumb to the diseases and dangers of the New World. For African captives, the New World was also a gamble, but one unwillingly taken and with much poorer odds.

> **The first stop for slaves was almost always one of the Caribbean ports or the mainland of South or Central America. (North Americans generally preferred to purchase slaves who had already worked a few years in the New World.) Slavery was a huge business at these ports of entry. Most slaves were purchased by speculators and wholesalers who expected to transport their merchandise to areas of demand and sell them at a profit.**

A dealer auctions off a family in a Charleston, South Carolina, marketplace. Africans who survived the horrors of the Middle Passage still had to endure the humiliation of being sold and the hardships of slave life.

Slaves were usually taken off the ship and put in special pens, which, while often crowded (the two main yards in Havana, Cuba, held 1,000 and 1,500 people respectively), were cleaner and roomier than the miserable ship holds of the Middle Passage. The captives were given plenty of food and encouraged to exercise; sickly or depressed slaves would fetch a lower price. Government officials frequently branded the slaves once they reached port to indicate that they had been legally imported; in some cases, purchasers would brand them as well.

> **Both newly imported captives and those who were being resold were auctioned off. Preceding the auction was a viewing period of several hours during which potential buyers inspected the slaves, judging their health and capacity for physical labor. Slave traders were notorious for concealing injuries, illnesses, or signs of advanced age. They would regularly clip off or dye gray hair; rub oil on the skin to conceal the ashy pallor caused by malnutrition or sickness; coach slaves as to how to answer certain questions; and even force them to dance, sing, or otherwise behave in a happy fashion. Because most purchasers knew about these tactics, their physical inspections were often humiliatingly thorough. Slaves were commonly stripped, pinched, and prodded. After the viewing period was over, the slaves were put on the auction block, either singly or in groups. The buyers then made their bids, and the highest bidder received the slave or slaves of his choice.**

Another method of selling newly imported Africans was called a scramble. During this process, slaves were offered in small groups or individually, but unlike the auction, each group or individual was sold at the same price. At a given signal, buyers—many of them wholesalers who planned to resell the people they bought—would race into the market area and claim the slaves they had selected. The noise and frenzied activity added to the miseries already heaped on the captives; as Olaudah Equiano put it, the scene "serve[d] not a little to increase the apprehensions of the terrified Africans." A few families, having managed to stay together during both the trek to the West African coast and the Middle Passage, might still be intact at this point. The scramble usually ended that. Because most buyers transported their purchases far from the point of sale, families separated at this stage stood little chance of ever reuniting.

After the slaves were sold, they were shipped to areas where their labor was needed. These journeys were much shorter than the Middle Passage, but they could be equally harsh. Blacks transported by ship were chained together in the hold, much as they had been during the Atlantic crossing. They received scant rations; a ship that carried slaves halfway around the island of Cuba, for example, provided each captive with one banana, two potatoes, and one small cup of water. Nineteenth-century slaves transported by railroad traveled in cattle cars along with cotton bales, livestock, tobacco, and other goods.

When there was no available route by sea, river, or railway, slaves walked to their destinations. To reach northern Colombia's Chocó mines from the Caribbean port of Cartagena, for example, slaves had to trek several hundred miles. Accompanied by armed, mounted guards, they carried heavy loads through lowland jungles and over the towering Andes Mountains. As a security measure, the guards chained them together by the hand or neck and forced them to walk single file. Exhaustion and disease often killed more

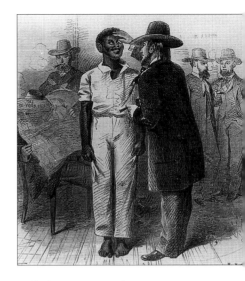

A dealer inspects a slave before purchasing him at an 1861 auction in Virginia. Slaves who did not attract buyers were often beaten after each unsuccessful auction.

than 20 percent of the slaves during this journey, a death rate just short of that for the Middle Passage.

Passing from middleman to planter or from one owner to another, slaves often had to move many times. Following the rigors of the Middle Passage, these frequent changes broke the health of many slaves and left them unfit for heavy physical labor. To counteract such effects, slave owners in the Caribbean and Latin America usually gave newly arrived Africans a respite from regular work, even trying to nurse the sick back to health. But if labor was scarce, the rest period was shortened or skipped altogether.

During their first few years in bondage, slaves underwent a process called "seasoning," a time when they learned what was expected of them as well as whatever mixed European-African language, called Creole, was spoken by the other slaves. Many also learned the language of their European overlords. Seasoning was not a gentle process; new slaves who showed signs of rebelliousness were flogged and tortured into submission. Masters regularly whipped them until they were covered in blood, and in the case of especially stubborn slaves, suspended them from trees or cropped their ears.

Many new slaves died during the seasoning process, succumbing to physical abuse, committing suicide, or simply failing to recover from the arduous transportation experience. But perhaps as many as half the deaths among newly arrived slaves were caused by disease. Although many Africans had already developed resistance to common tropical diseases such as malaria or yellow fever (which also proved deadly to whites), European diseases such as pneumonia, influenza, and whooping cough were new to them. These afflictions ravaged the African population. The Caribbean, because of its role as a center of trade and its high volume of ship traffic, was especially plagued by new diseases, including cholera brought by traders from Asia.

Insufficient rations caused many slaves to die of malnutrition, and large numbers perished from dysentery and other ailments brought on by unsanitary living conditions. The death rate for newly arrived Africans was as high as 30 percent

A large, heavy metal collar thwarts a would-be runaway. Such devices were used during the process known as seasoning and were designed to break the spirit of new slaves.

A poster advertising human beings for sale in South Carolina repeatedly assures buyers that the captives do not have smallpox. Although smallpox caused fewer deaths among Africans than among Native Americans, other diseases were equally fatal.

in some areas. Historian Eric Williams (in his 1970 book *From Columbus to Castro: The History of the Caribbean, 1492–1969*) determined that in the West Indies from 1715 to 1775, 44 out of every 100 enslaved Africans died either in transport or during their first three years of bondage.

Africans who lived through the first years of slavery still suffered from malnutrition, illness, and abuse. In many of the New World colonies, the slave population was never self-sustaining. In other words, slaves were not able to survive in large enough numbers to maintain or increase their total population. Owners and overseers felt it was cheaper to work slaves to death and buy new ones than to provide existing slaves with decent conditions. High death rates created a continuous demand for slaves that spurred the slave trade, a vicious cycle that claimed hundreds of thousands of African lives. According to Eric Williams,

> After eight years of [slave] importations, averaging 4,424 a year, the population of Barbados was only 3,411 larger. 35,397 slaves had been imported; 31,897 had disappeared. In 1770 and 1771 the mortality was so high that the importation in those years, heavy though it was, was not adequate to supply the deficit. Half the population had to be renewed in eight years.
>
> The total population [of Jamaica] in 1778, excluding births and based only on imports, should have been 541,893, and that figure excludes imports for 1776, 1777 and 1778. Allowing 11,000 a year for those three years, the total population in 1778 should have been 547,893. The actual population in that year was less than 40 per cent of the potential total.

Not all the colonies had such high death rates, and in some parts of Jamaica and Barbados death rates were fairly low. But all the New World colonies and nations contained regions that consumed slaves, constantly requiring new imports to maintain the laboring population. The type of work demanded of the slaves was more important than any other factor in determining their fate. For example, slaves in Spanish colonies such as Cuba had in theory extensive legal protection, while the United States had few laws to protect slaves. But due to the differences in the sort of labor required from slaves, the U.S. slave population had increased from an estimated 430,000 to approximately 4.5 million, most of them American-born, in 1863; Cuba, on the other hand, had to import Africans constantly simply to maintain its slave population.

Large, profitable operations—sugar plantations in the Caribbean, coffee plantations in Brazil, and cotton plantations in the United States—were usually the deadliest locales for slaves (although certain types of mining were also dangerous). Such plantations usually contained a large number of slaves, comparatively few white overseers, and an owner who was generally removed from the day-to-day activities of his property. Some owners even lived in distant cities or in Europe. They often pressured their overseers to maximize profits and rarely supervised their treatment of slaves; as a result, overseers commonly overworked their charges. In order to increase production even more, slaves on large plantations were usually denied free time to grow food crops and were forced to depend on notoriously poor plantation rations. To shave costs, overseers often supplied slaves with inadequate housing, clothing, and food, and few provided facilities for any sort of leisure activity.

Because they were far outnumbered by black slaves, white overseers and owners lived in constant fear of rebellions, and they responded cruelly to the slightest sign of defiance. In 1736, for example, whites on the Caribbean island of Antigua became convinced that slaves were plotting to exterminate them. Masters began to torture and bribe slaves to implicate themselves and others, and by the time the scare was over, they had executed 88 blacks. Of these, 77 were burned at the stake, 5 broken on the rack, and 6 suspended in steel cages called gibbets until they died from exposure.

Even slaves in areas where conditions were not so harsh were always at risk of being "sold down the river" to a worse site. High death rates and resulting labor shortages on large plantations gave rise to a bustling internal slave trade as traders snapped up surplus slaves from small

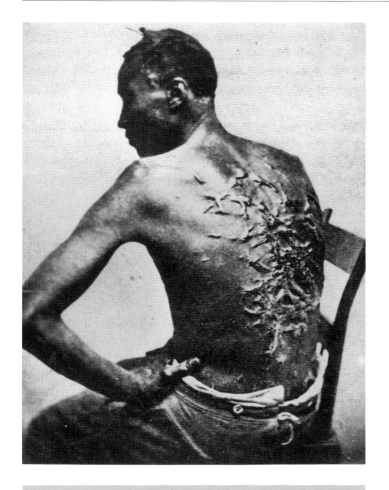

An enslaved man from a cotton plantation in Louisiana displays his scars, the result of a whipping, in this 1863 photograph.

farms and towns and transported them to areas of demand. In the United States, enterprising slave owners in the smaller, more northerly plantations, where death rates were comparatively low, even began slave-breeding programs. Breeders forced female slaves to reproduce and supply more human beings for the cotton and sugar plantations of the Deep South, where death rates were extremely high.

Owners sometimes used the resale as a punishment. James W. C. Pennington, a fugitive slave who later became a minister, described in his 1850 memoir, *The Fugitive Blacksmith, or Events in the History of James W. C. Pennington,* how a certain slave owner "when he thought it necessary to secure unqualified obedience . . . would strike a slave with any weapon, flog him on the bare back, and sell." Any resale could break up whatever family a slave had managed to establish. In *Narratives of the Sufferings of Lewis and Milton Clarke* (1846), former slave Lewis Clarke maintained:

> *I never knew a whole family to live together till all were grown up, in my life.* There is almost always, in every family, some one or more keen and bright, or else sullen and stubborn slave, whose influence they are afraid of on the rest of the family, and such a one must take a walking ticket to the south.
>
> There are other causes of separation. The death of a large owner is the occasion usually of many families being broken up. Bankruptcy is another cause of separation, and the hard-heartedness of a majority of slaveholders another and more fruitful cause than either or all the rest.

No matter what the circumstances, the life of a slave was precisely that—a life where a person had almost no legal rights or control over his or her own destiny. Even in areas where mortality was low and the chance of legal manumission relatively good, escapes and revolts occurred frequently (often to the amazement of the slave owners). As William Craft recalled in his mid-19th-century book, *Running a Thousand Miles for Freedom, or the Escape of William and Ellen Craft from Slavery:*

> It is true, our condition as slaves was not by any means the worst; but the mere idea that we were held as chattels, and deprived of all legal rights—the thought that we had to give up our hard earning to a tyrant, to enable him to live in idleness and luxury—the thought that we could not call

the bones and sinews that God gave us our own: but above all, the fact that another man had the power to tear from our cradle the new-born babe and sell it in the shambles [market] like a brute, and then scourge us if we dared to lift a finger to save it from such a fate, haunted us for years.

And most rebellious slaves probably shared the feelings of abolitionist leader Frederick Douglass, who recounted in his *Narrative of the Life of Frederick Douglass* (1845) his own decision to escape slavery:

> In coming to a fixed determination to run away, we did more than [U.S. patriot] Patrick Henry, when he resolved upon liberty or death. With us it was a doubtful liberty at most, and almost certain death if we failed. For my part, I should prefer death to hopeless bondage.

Slave dealers drag a newly sold boy away from his mother. "A slaveholder never appears to me so completely an agent of hell," wrote ex-slave Frederick Douglass, "as when I think of and look upon my dear children."

7

THE END OF THE TRADE

Some Europeans had opposed the slave trade from the start. The sufferings of the Middle Passage were no secret, and even people who were not particularly opposed to slavery itself were disturbed by the brutalities of the Atlantic crossing. American patriot and future U.S. president Thomas Jefferson, himself a slave owner, even included a denunciation of British slave trading in an early draft of the Declaration of Independence. The passage, which was unacceptable to the southern delegates of the Continental Congress and ultimately removed, read in part:

> He [King George III of Britain] has waged cruel war against human nature itself, violating its most sacred rights of life and liberty in the persons of a distant people who never offended him, captivating and carrying them into slavery in another hemisphere, or to incur miserable death in their transportation thither.

By the early 1770s, the British were conducting most of the world's slave trade. After the United States declared its independence in 1776, however, the Brit-

A specialized New Orleans slave market offers trained maids, cooks, butlers, and coach drivers, some fetching up to $800. Although the United States outlawed the importation of slaves in 1808, the domestic slave trade continued for almost 60 years more.

Thomas Jefferson, the third president of the United States, watches a slave work outside Monticello, his Virginia estate. Although Jefferson owned slaves (and freed only a handful of them), he was firmly committed to the abolition of the slave trade.

ish government no longer directly profited from slave labor in North America. And by 1798, fully half of all slaves transported by the British were being sold to French Caribbean colonies whose products (mainly sugar) competed directly with those from the British Caribbean colonies. British public opinion was also turning against slavery. In 1787, a number of high-ranking Britons organized the Society for Effecting the Abolition of the Slave Trade, and parliamentary hearings in 1788 on the misery and mortality aboard slave ships provided a publicity bonanza for the trade's opponents. In 1807, Great Britain officially abolished the African slave trade.

In spite of Britain's prohibition, traders from other nations as well as pirates from England itself continued to pursue the African slave trade for decades. And although the United States banned the importation of slaves in 1808, it was still going on as late as 1860, when U.S. authorities captured 12 ships carrying 3,119 Africans. Captives illegally brought to the New World often endured worse conditions during the Middle Passage than those brought earlier.

Every time a slaver made an illegal Atlantic run he risked being caught and, in some areas, being executed for piracy. To reduce the number of these hazardous trips, slavers crammed in even more people. They also attempted to conceal their captives by keeping them below decks at all times or by crowding them in among the barrels and casks that made up the ship's legal cargo. When pursued by authorities, slavers often pitched their captives into the ocean to avoid being caught with them.

Determined to curb this traffic, Great Britain began to pressure other governments to outlaw it. Spain gave in first, agreeing to abolish the trade in an 1820 treaty with Great Britain. In some instances, Britain resorted to force. In the late 1840s and early 1850s, its navy attacked Brazilian slave ships and threatened to blockade Brazilian ports unless Brazil ended the importation of Africans. Britain's enemies believed that the navy's antislavery measures were simply an excuse to demonstrate its dominance of the world's oceans. Consequently, anti-British officials aided illegal slavers whenever they could, regarding such acts as well-earned slaps at British arrogance. Ultimately, only the abolition of slavery itself would end the importation of captives.

Nonetheless, the official abolition of the slave trade greatly reduced the number of new slaves imported into most areas of the Americas. The reduction indirectly improved conditions for slaves already there: because the price of Africans rose, owners had a financial incentive for taking care of the ones they had. But old habits died hard, and change came slowly in some places. In Jamaica, where the African slave trade was cut off in 1808, the slave population did not begin to increase naturally until the 1840s. In Brazil, the slave population was never self-sustaining. In an 1868 article, "The Extinction of Slavery in Brazil, from a Practical Point of View," British explorer Sir Richard Burton wrote that the high death rate among slaves, combined with the stoppage of new African imports, would achieve the end of Brazilian slavery long before any abolitionist crusade could do it.

Ending the African slave trade, of course, could not alter the past. Millions of unwilling people had been transported from one continent to another to work as laborers. This forced migration had profound effects on the culture and history of three continents: Africa and North and South America. Africa, not surprisingly, was seriously weakened by the slave trade. The more than 10 million Africans snatched from their homeland had been those who would bring high prices: healthy, physically strong people between the ages of 10 and 30—the same people who would have become the continent's leading warriors, builders, farmers, and parents. Their disappearance caused massive social disruptions, as

A slave dealership in 19th-century Alexandria, Virginia, baldly advertises its wares. Despite attempts to end the importation of slaves from Africa, smugglers found a ready market as long as slavery existed.

did the Europeans' introduction of the gun. And, as the slave trade spread, African internal warfare worsened.

The trade also changed the European view of Africa. In their first contacts, Europeans had regarded Africans as equal trading partners. When the slave trade reached its peak, however, Europeans justified it by labeling Africans inferior beings who were naturally fit to serve white men. It was this attitude that helped spur the European conquest of Africa in the late 19th century.

As Africa declined through the slave trade, Europe prospered. Although there is considerable disagreement concerning the extent of slavery's effect on the European economy, it was undeniably a positive one. Many families made great fortunes, and certain cities (Bristol and Liverpool in Great Britain; Nantes and Bordeaux in France) prospered immensely by fitting out ships and providing sailors for the trade. Of perhaps greater importance to the European economy was the sizable African market for such manufactured goods as cloth, metalwork, and firearms. African demand for these products spurred the growth of factories in Great Britain and France, permanently altering and enlarging their economies.

> **In the Americas, the effects of slavery would be even more complex. Captured Africans brought along their religions, languages, and traditions, which (like those of countless other immigrants) wove themselves into the New World's developing culture. In mid-19th century Brazil, for example, a group of Muslim slaves battled for and won both their freedom and their right to worship in their own chosen way. Heading for Brazil's wild interior, the rebels established an Islamic community that still exists in the state of Bahia. Non-Muslim African religious traditions are reflected in a variety of present-day New World religions, including Voodoo and Santeria.**

African oral traditions have deeply influenced the literatures of the Americas; certain popular stories, such as the Uncle Remus tales in the United States, can be traced to specific West African folk tales. African languages have also left their mark on New World speech; among the African-derived everyday words in American English are *gumbo* and *banjo*. And the influence of African traditions on a wide variety of New World music, including jazz, ragtime, reggae, gospel, calypso, and rock and roll, is widely documented.

Africans were also essential to the New World's economic development. Typical is the progress of rice cultivation in the southern United States, which is in many ways a history of African agricultural genius. On the advice of slaves who had cultivated the crop at home, Virginia settlers began planting rice in 1648. Skilled farmers, imported specifically from African areas of rice cultivation, showed their masters how to turn marshlands into paddy fields and how to design the complex irrigation networks

The House of Representatives explodes into cheers with the passage of the 13th Amendment, which abolished slavery in the United States almost a century after the country achieved independence.

Southern "gentlemen" punish a free black man for trying to exercise his rights. Racists continued to persecute African Americans long after the abolition of slavery.

demanded by rice. The grain eventually became a major cash crop in South Carolina and Georgia; not surprisingly, these two states fiercely opposed abolishing the slave trade, which supplied them with these valuable farmers.

Slavery also left a lasting political legacy. Its abolition was a major goal of the many South and Central American colonial independence movements; when these colonies became free nations, they freed all the slaves at once. But the economic and agricultural systems developed during slavery could not be so easily ended. Under the slave system, most land was owned by wealthy people who neglected food production in favor of cultivating such cash crops as cotton and tobacco. Ownership patterns did not always change with abolition, and for many slaves, liberation only meant the freedom to become poor, hungry, and landless. Land distribution and the rights of poor farmers became explosive (and continuing) political issues in much of South and Central America.

Slavery deeply influenced the history of the growing United States, most obviously in the conflicts between the North and the South that would lead to the bloody Civil War. Caribbean slavery also made its mark on the North American republic: the 1791 slave rebellion in the French colony of Santo Domingo (part of the island of Hispaniola) gave birth to the independent nation of Haiti and forced France to abandon its hopes for a New World empire. Thus in 1803, France sold to the United States the enormous Louisiana Territory, from which parts or all of 12 states—Louisiana, Texas, Arkansas, Missouri, Kansas, Iowa, Nebraska, North and South Dakota, Oklahoma, Minnesota, and Montana—would be carved.

But no matter what happened in the rest of the New World, U.S. citizens continued to enslave people of African descent until 1865, when the Civil War ended and the 13th Amendment to the Constitution was ratified. But racism did not die with the abolition of slavery. It lived on in a variety of laws and customs designed to keep blacks from obtaining their full benefits as citizens. African Americans would have to face many more years of battle before securing the rights, liberties, and freedoms guaranteed by their native land.

FURTHER READING

Bennett, Lerone, Jr. *Before the Mayflower: A History of Black America, 1619–1964*. Baltimore, MD: Penguin Books, 1984.

Bontemps, Arna, ed. *Great Slave Narratives*. Boston: Beacon Press, 1969.

Davidson, Basil. *Black Mother: The Years of the African Slave Trade*. Boston: Atlantic Monthly Press, 1961.

———, ed. *The African Past: Chronicles from Antiquity to Modern Times*. Boston: Atlantic Monthly Press, 1964.

Dodge, Stephen C. *Christopher Columbus and the First Voyages to the New World*. New York: Chelsea House, 1991.

Duncan, Alice Smith. *Sir Francis Drake and the Struggle for an Ocean Empire*. New York: Chelsea House, 1993.

Franklin, John Hope. *From Slavery to Freedom: A History of Negro Americans*. 6th ed. New York: Knopf, 1987.

Greene, Lorenzo J. *The Negro in Colonial New England*. New York: Atheneum, 1968.

Kolchin, Peter. *American Slavery: 1619–1877*. New York: Hill and Wang, 1993.

Lester, Julius. *To Be a Slave*. New York: Dial Press, 1968.

Rawley, James A. *The Transatlantic Slave Trade: A History*. New York: Norton, 1981.

Rice, C. Duncan. *The Rise and Fall of Black Slavery*. New York: Harper and Row, 1975.

Steffof, Rebecca. *Vasco da Gama and the Portuguese Explorers*. New York: Chelsea House, 1993.

INDEX

ANDREW K. FRANK, a graduate of Brandeis University, received his M.A. in history from the University of Florida, where he is currently pursuing his Ph.D. in American history. His next project involves the cultural frontier in the colonial South.

DARLENE CLARK HINE, senior consulting editor of the MILESTONES IN BLACK AMERICAN HISTORY series, is the John A. Hannah Professor of American History at Michigan State University. She is the author of numerous books and articles on black women's history, as well as the editor of the two-volume *Black Women in America: An Historical Encyclopedia* (1993). Her most recent work is *Hine Sight: Black Women and the Re-Construction of American History*.

CLAYBORNE CARSON, senior consulting editor of the MILESTONES IN BLACK AMERICAN HISTORY series, is a professor of history at Stanford University. His first book, *In Struggle: SNCC and the Black Awakening of the 1960s* (1981), won the Frederick Jackson Turner Prize of the Organization of American Historians. He is the director of the Martin Luther King, Jr., Papers Project, which will publish 12 volumes of King's writings.

PICTURE CREDITS